BEAU-HE-ME-N-RIB

MARY-SUSAN
KIRKPATRICK

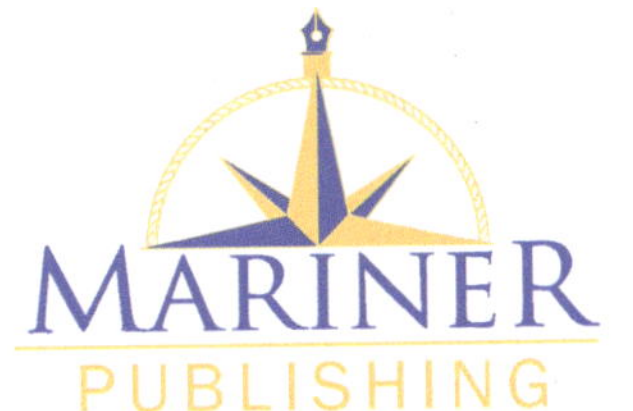

Library of Congress Control Number: 2008933391

Beau-He-Me-N-Rib
Mary-Susan Kirkpatrick

p. cm.

1. Contemporary American Art—Acrylic Painting
2. Contemporary American Art—Ceramics
3. Spiritual—Poetry
4. American Poetry—20th Century
5. American Poetry—21st Century
6. Christian—Poetry

I. Kirkpatrick, Mary-Susan II. Title
ISBN 13: 978-0-9820172-0-3 (softcover : alk. paper)
ISBN 13: 978-0-9820172-2-7 (casebound: alk. paper)

1 3 5 7 9 10 8 6 4 2

Photography by Bruce Young
Book design by Jennifer Law Young and Mary-Susan Kirkpatrick

Mariner Publishing
A division of
Mariner Companies, Inc.
131 West 21st St.
Buena Vista, VA 24416
Tel: 540-264-0021
http://www.MarinerMedia.com
Printed in the United States of America

This book is printed on acid-free paper meeting the requirements of the American Standard for Permanence of Paper for Printed Library Materials.

Cover painting "The Blessing" by author.

THANKSGIVING TO GOD
LOVE TO MY MOTHER AND FATHER
MARY ANN AND TOM
MY BROTHERS TREY AND PETER
AND ESPECIALLY MORRISON,
SCHÖN, PIERRE, AND SAMMY GREY

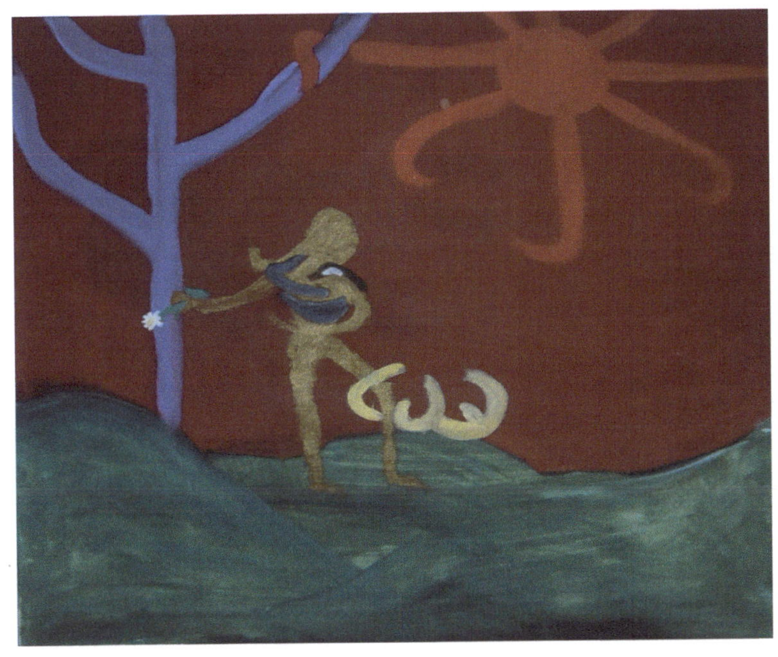

I loved being a 70's child. The halcyon aura allowed me to be who I am today. Richmond, Virginia was a great southern city to grow up in. Culturally there was a lot to offer and I was located between the Atlantic Ocean and the Blue Ridge Mountains.

My parents were high school sweethearts from Lexington, Virginia. My father's Scotch-Irish ancestors settled in Rockbridge County in 1750. One of my paternal great-grandfathers, Samuel Morrison Wilbourn, was the originator and first manufacturer of the Wilbourn Patent Saddle also known as the Buena Vista Saddle. His wife Eliza Trotter Wilbourn, taught art at Southern Seminary. My mother's side called Lexington home since the 1930's.

I was the youngest of three children. My two older brothers helped make growing up a fun adventure. Trey majored in ocean engineering. This was not a surprise for the Kirkpatrick family as much as we love the water. Peter was knighted in the Order of Arts and Letters by the French Ambassador to the United States. I was fortunate that they had excellent taste in classic rock music and they both accumulated a well appreciated collection of albums. Since a young girl I painted with these songs in the background and still do to this day.

Painting has always been natural for me. I feel blessed visually expressing what I am feeling and showing my personal life journey. The spirit of the American Indian is a subject that I have concentrated painting since my early years. When I connect with someone instantly they are American Indian including my childhood friend whose love for animals is equal to mine. Past the continental United States my heart has also been drawn towards Alaska's Yupik and Inupiat tribes and the Canadian Inuit and Inuinnaq.

Since 1993, after college I have been traveling throughout the United States and internationally. Over the years I have met some gentle souls that have touched my life with their kindness including friends from Nepal, Indonesia, Thailand, and China. While I had the time being in their presence I noticed laughter is what we enjoyed the most. No matter what different religious background, we all want the same things in life: health and joy. My friends and I discussed how our belief in our faith is what strengthens us each and every day.

When I think of happiness I think of the animals that have been in my life. My dog Morrison's personality always keeps a smile on my face and he loves to travel with me! The ocean also keeps me in a positive state of mind. I would live in the ocean instead of by the ocean if it was possible. I always loved to swim out in the Atlantic.....far out.....and the dolphins were next to me gracefully on their way to their destination.

During my preteens surfing began to show up in my artwork . I was always in awe of the big wave riders. Surfing in Hawaii was a time that I never wanted to end. One of the best surfers on this planet was right there guiding me, along with a stunning view of the sea turtles. I also like snowboarding......another rush in itself.

Growing up, writing poetry was always something that I liked to do. Sometimes the poems turn out lighthearted—other times more serious. While working on my paintings in the studio I write poems to go along with each one. Writing song lyrics began in the sixth grade and it continues.

Creating art comes from my innermost being. I am here on this earth to express what makes me, Mary-Susan Kirkpatrick, an individual. My emotions of the heart are painted on canvas and shaped from clay. Love is what allows me to show the spiritual dance I am feeling within.

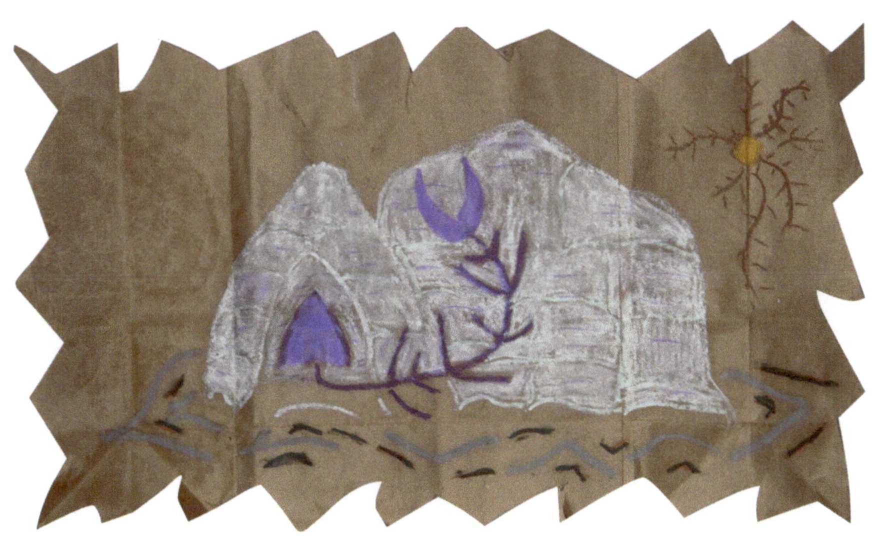

PAINT

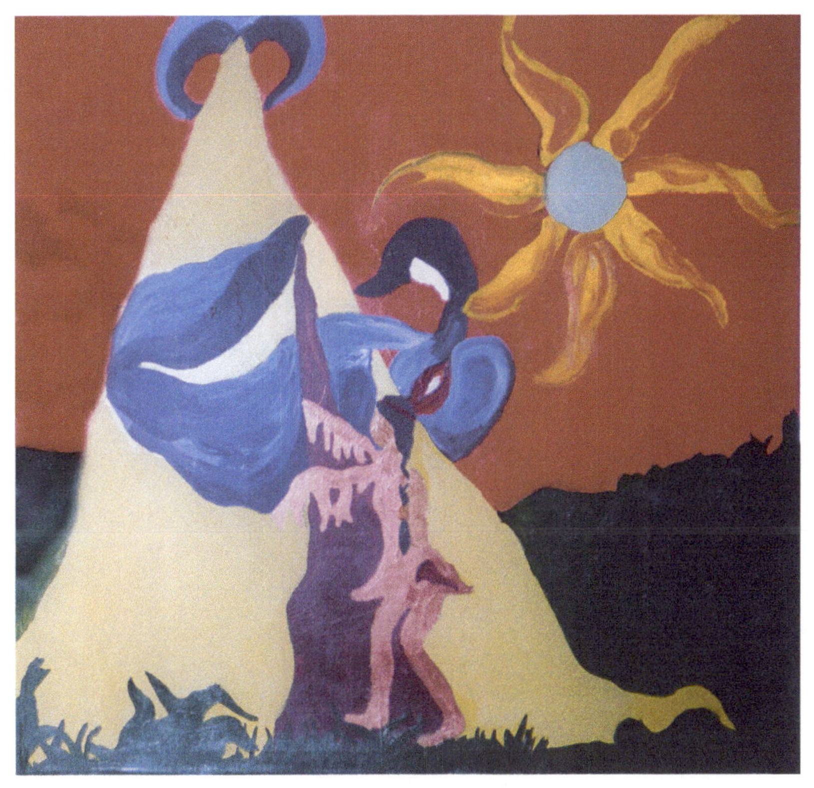

Paint and clay
the view of my life
where I am in control
Jophiel
the angel of creativity
understands
this is how I express my soul

Jophiel
1995
Acrylic on canvas
48 x 36 in

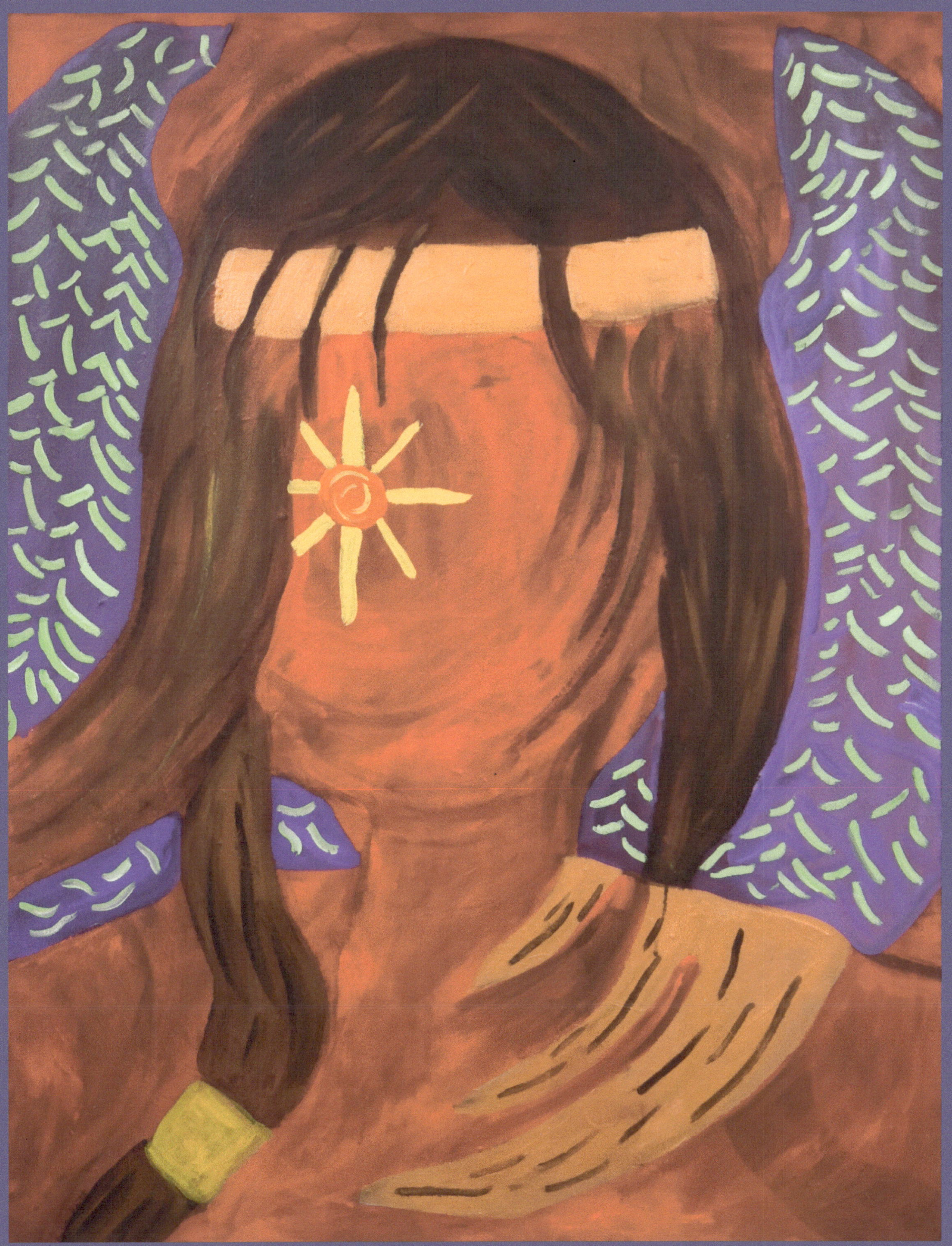

THOUGHT ABOUT WITH DEEP PRECISION
THE DAUGHTER OF JOACHIM AND ANN
WAS THE DECISION

THE DECISION
1993
ACRYLIC ON CANVAS
42 X 36 IN

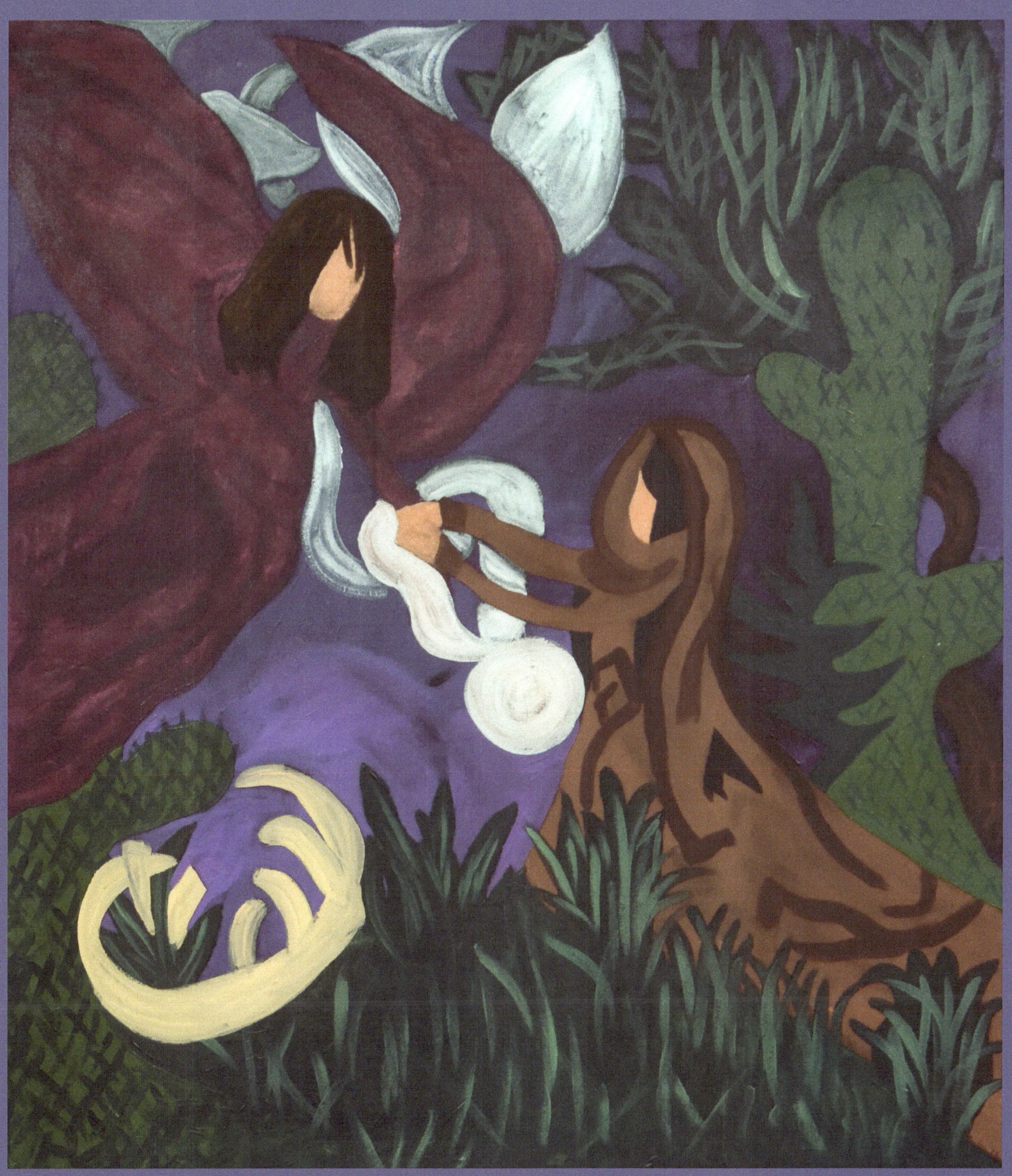

VEIL FLOWS OVER JOSEPH
THE BRAVE WOMAN
ONCE KNOWN AS THE CHOSEN GIRL
THEY HOLD IN THEIR HANDS
THE POWER OF THE PEARL

POWER OF THE PEARL
2000
ACRYLIC ON CANVAS
50 X 46 IN

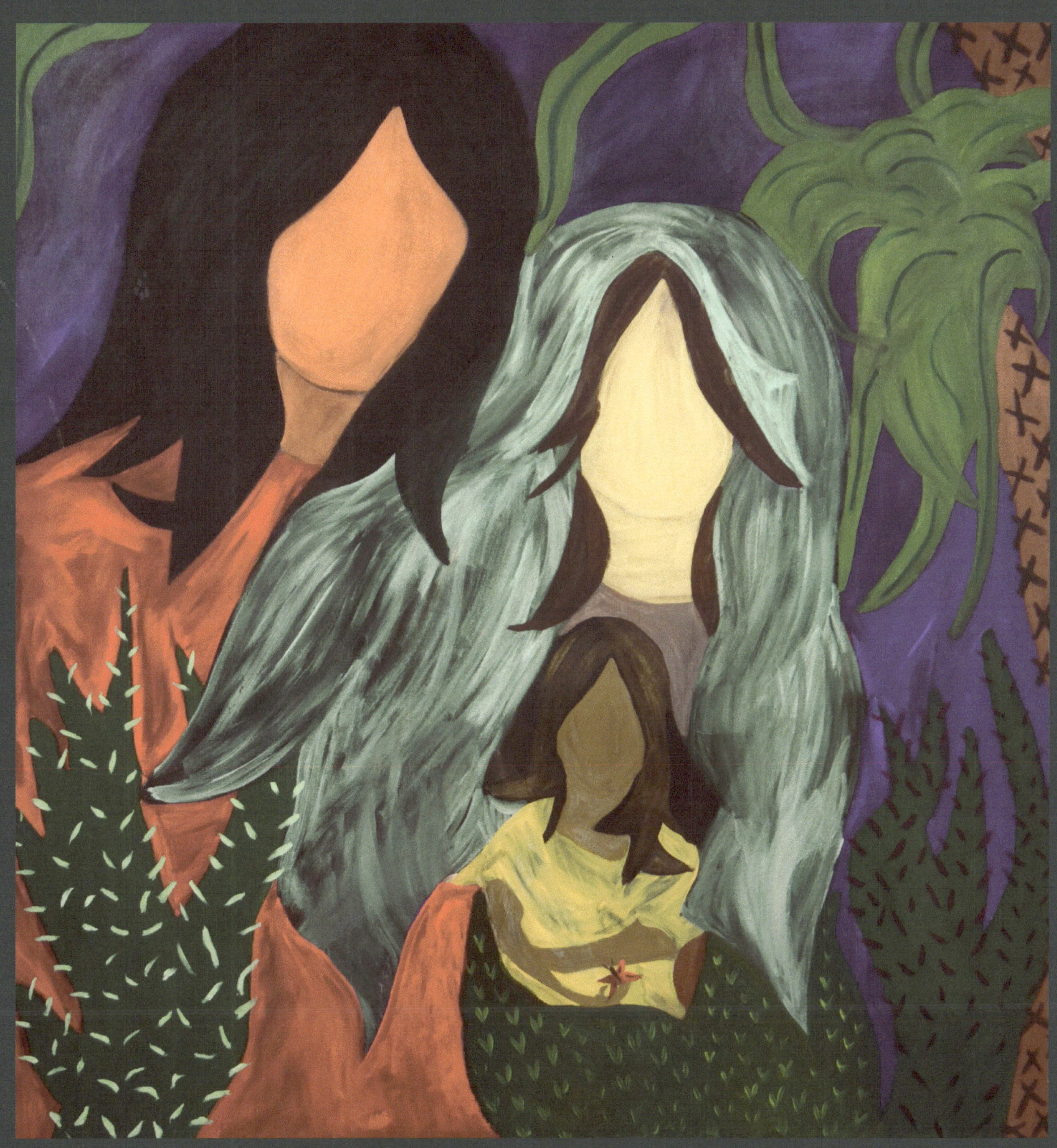

MARTHA, MARTHA
ENTERTAINING
BUSY ALL DAY
LET US STOP TO REMEMBER
IT IS ALWAYS A GOOD TIME TO PRAY

MARTHA, MARTHA
1993
ACRYLIC ON CANVAS
42 X 36 IN

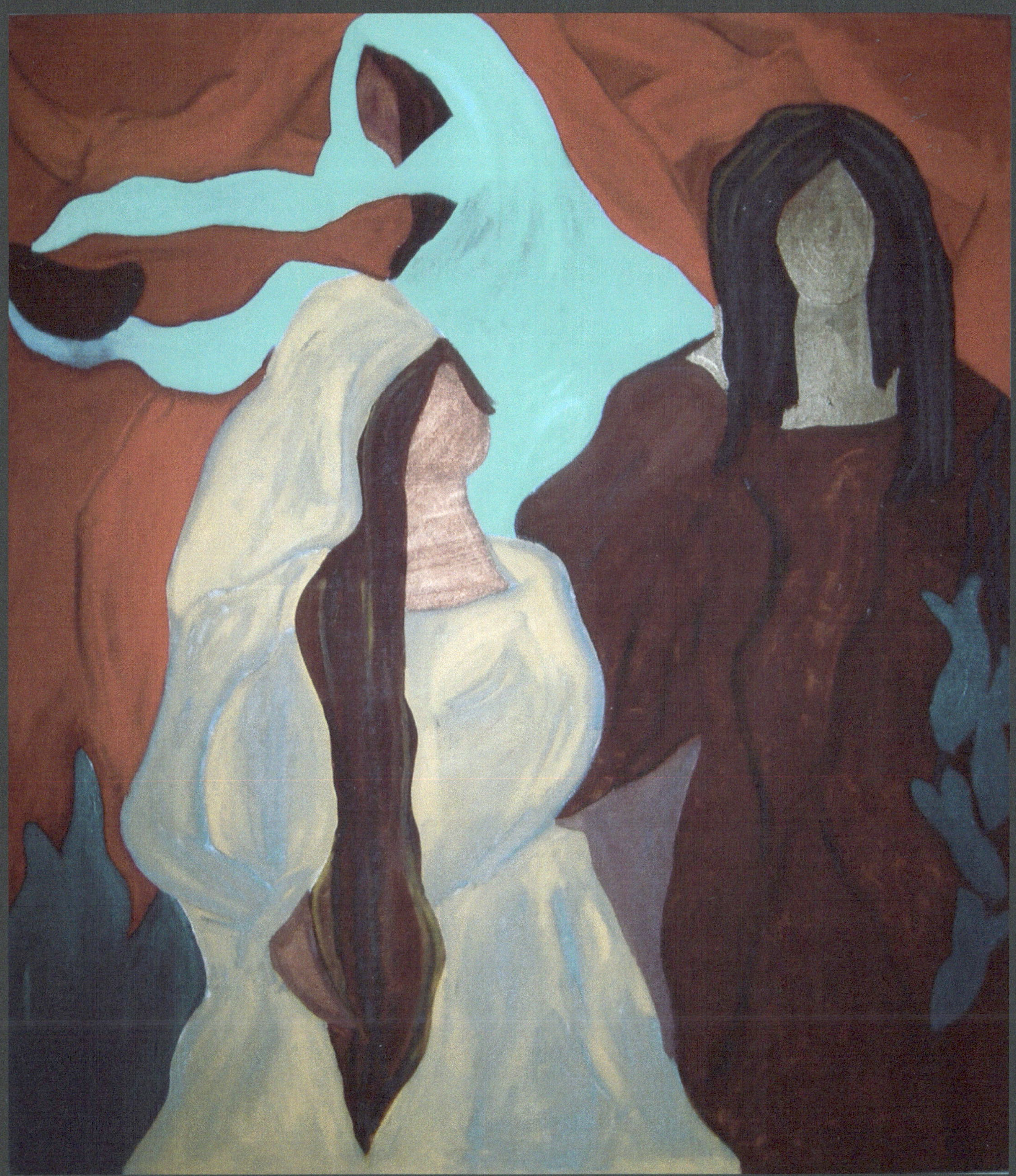

His family
his friends
the tears they shed and how they cried
trying to remain strong
our sins
the reason he died
hours past
sun disappeared a few times
the sign of a morning ray
it was then they rejoiced
the vision they saw
he had risen for them on the third day

THE THIRD DAY
2003
ACRYLIC ON CANVAS
49 X 42 IN

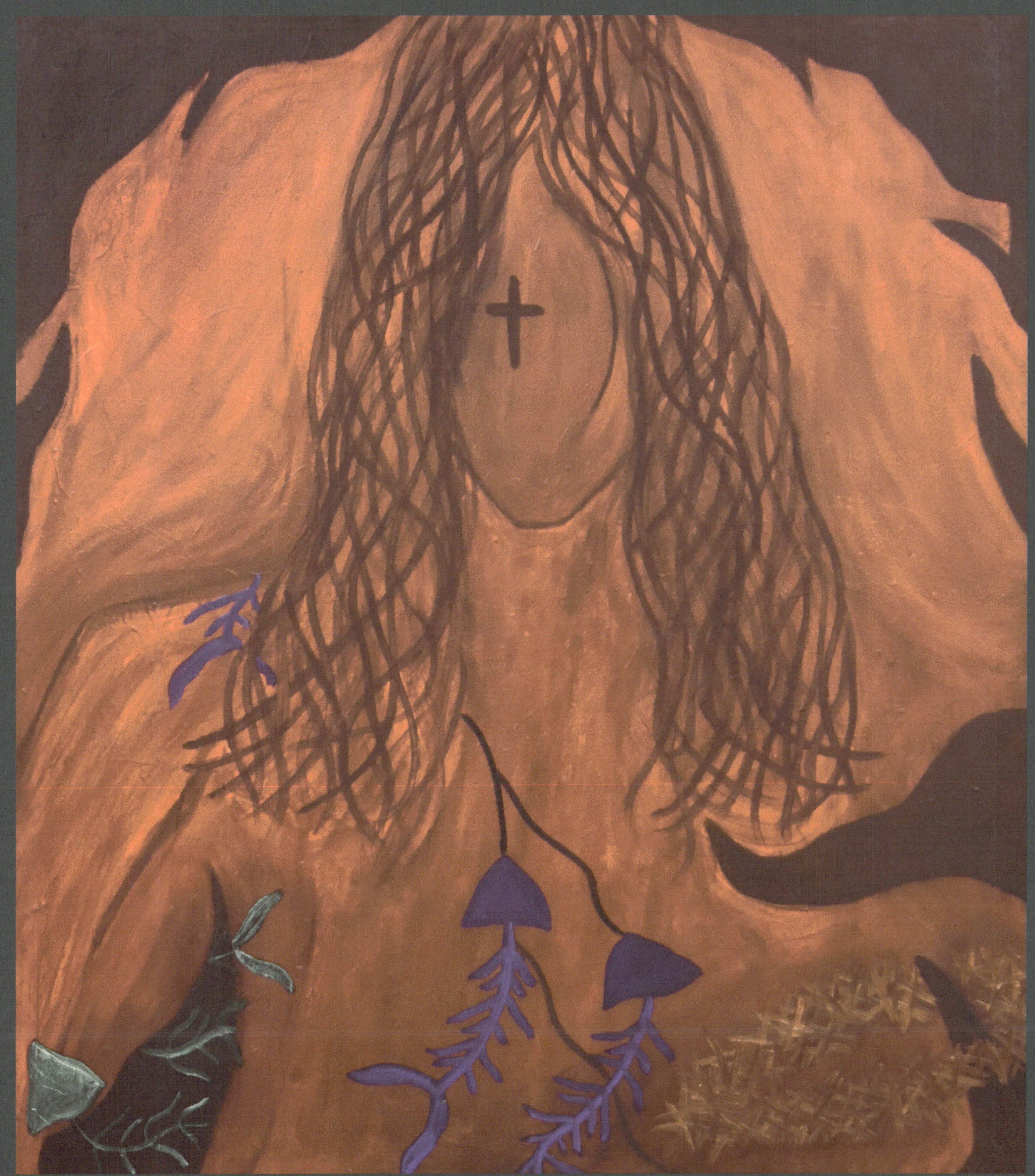

HE IS NEVER TO BE SEEN BY THE VISIBLE EYE
THERE ARE SOME WHO HAVE GIVEN IT A TRY
BORN WITH FINS ARE THE ONLY ONE HE CONFIDES IN
THOSE WHO LIVE ON THE EDGE OF POSEIDON

THE EDGE OF POSEIDON
1991
ACRYLIC ON CANVAS
40 X 31 IN

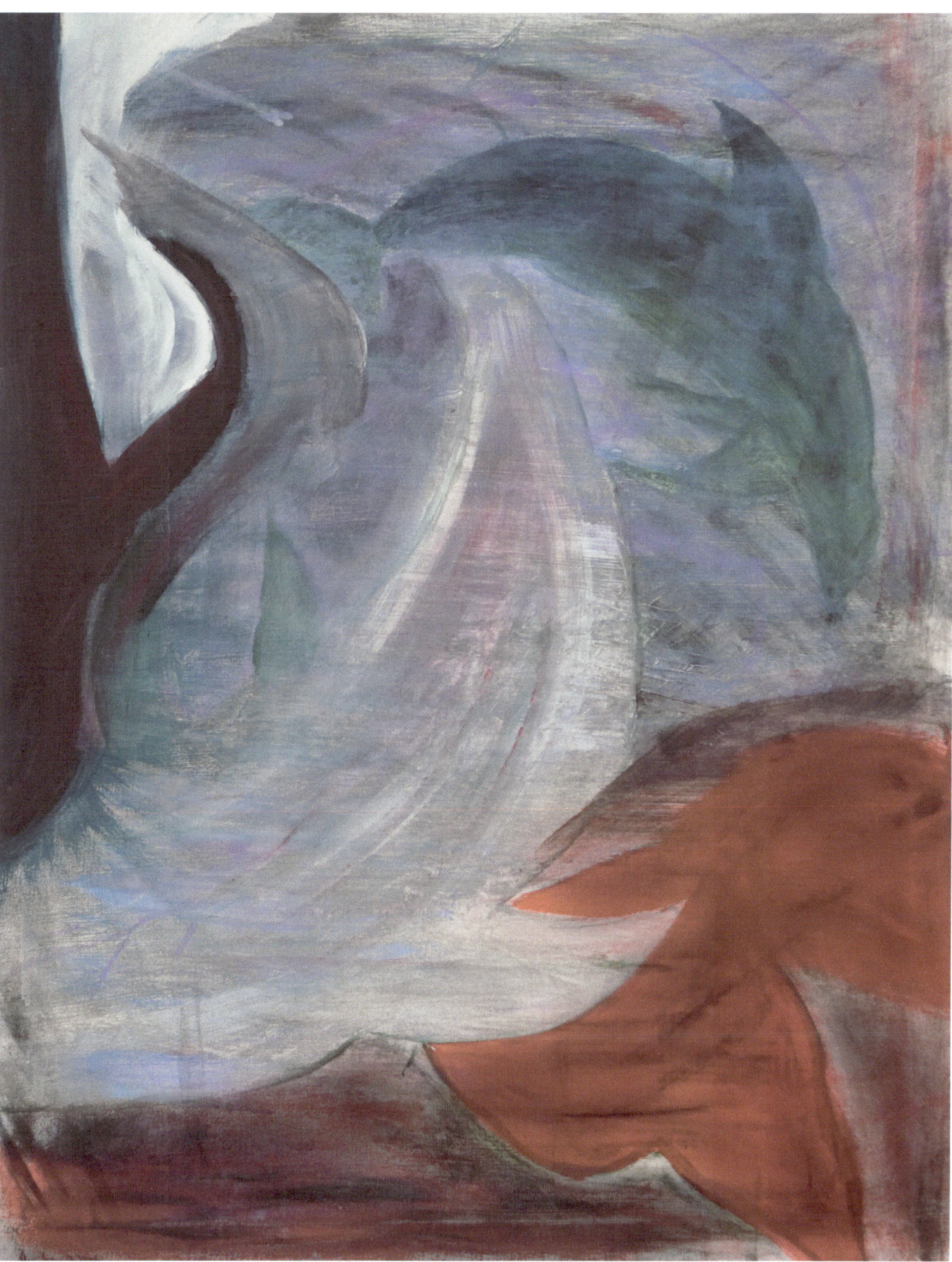

SOUTHERN WISHES
FOREVER I SEND
WHERE THE JOURNEY OF THE DOLPHIN
HAS NO END

NALU
1993
ACRYLIC ON CANVAS
42 X 36 IN

SENIOR STUDIO THESIS EXHIBITION
HUNT-CAVANAGH GALLERY
SPRING 1993

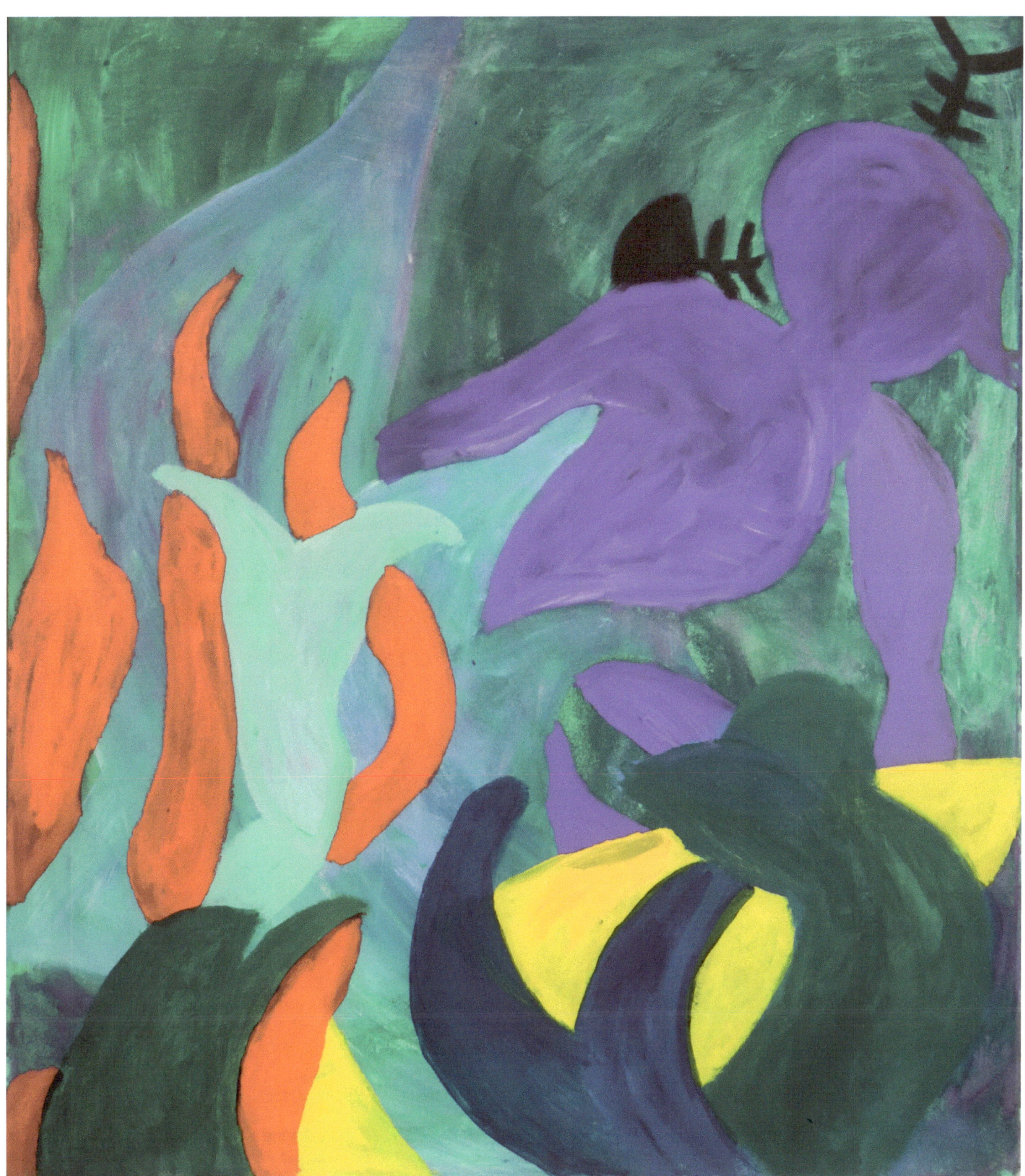

Never a moment dull
from the genius mind encased in your skull

Immersed
2007
Acrylic on canvas
53 x 15 in

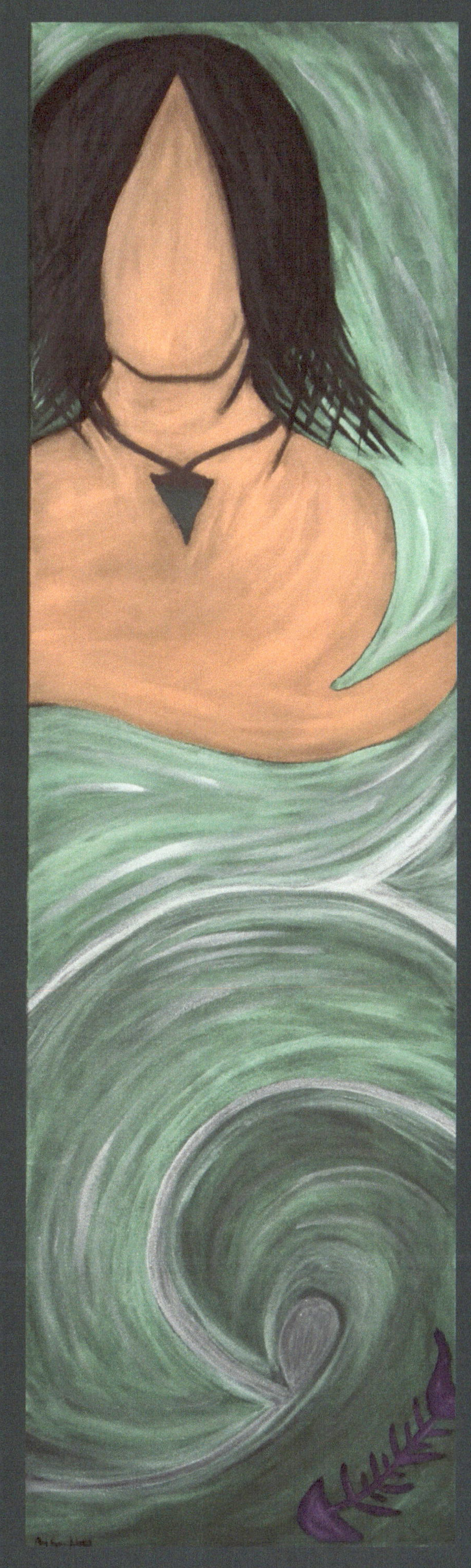

Drenched in salt water
the body did crave
his soul hoping to be one with the wave
the surfboard patiently balanced in hand
the anticipation as he stood in the sand
the breeze invited him in as a few palms from the tree fell
then he gratefully accepted when he approved of the swell

Rarotonga
2004
Acrylic on canvas
48 X 36 in

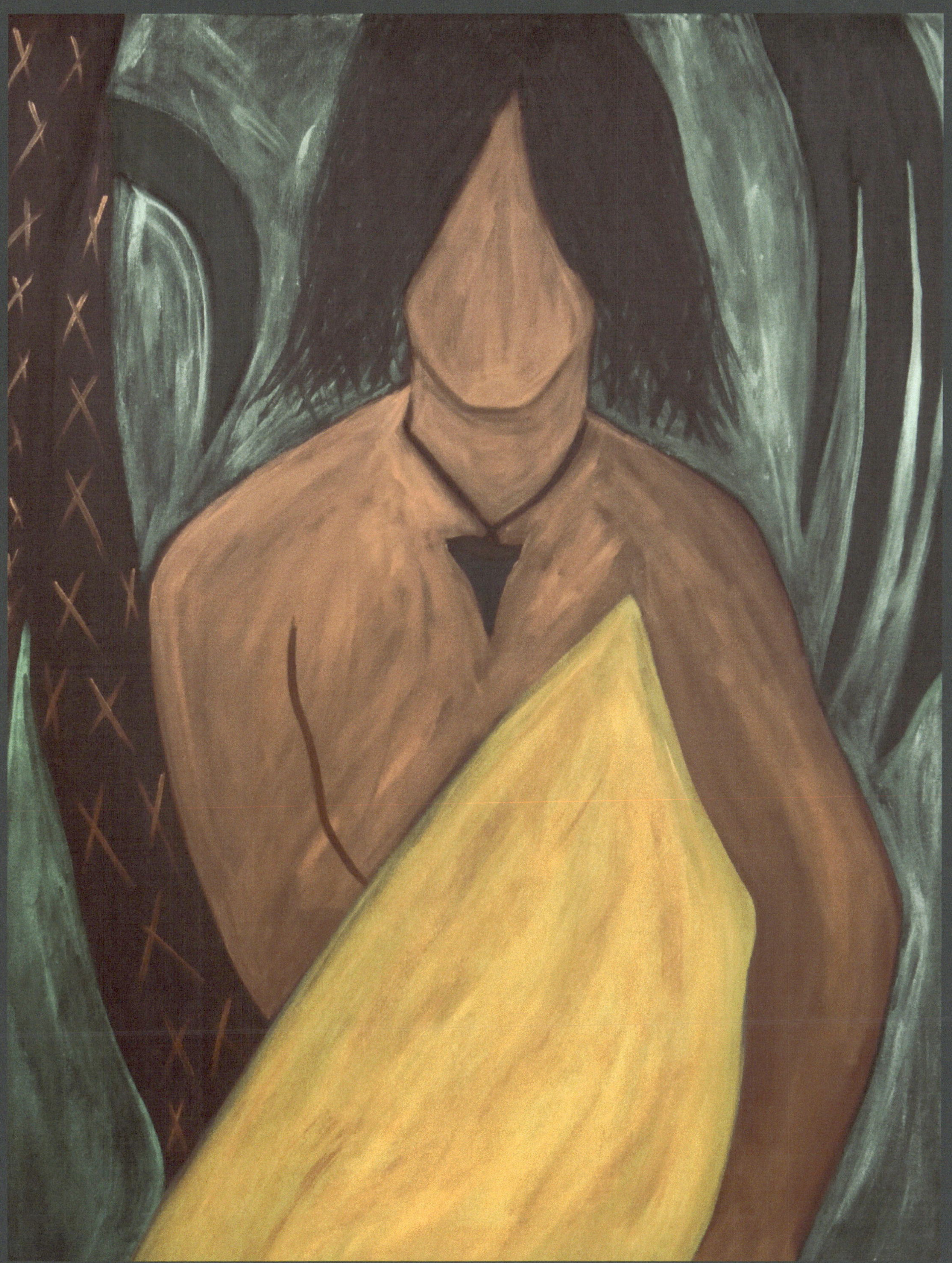

YOU WANTED TO KNOW IF WE SHOULD ELOPE
HOW ABOUT ROME? BORROW THE POPE?
WE COULD RUN OFF TO SANTA FE
HIDE IN AN ADOBE FAR AWAY
HOW ABOUT ALASKA?
BUILD AN IGLOO OF ICE
OR GO TO CHINA
WATCH THE PANDAS
DO YOU PREFER INDICA OR JAPONICA RICE?
SHOULD WE CATCH THE MOTHER SHIP TO OUTER SPACE?
LEAVE THIS PLANET WITHOUT A TRACE
WHEREVER WE GO IT WILL BE ENCHANTED
AS LONG AS WE DO NOT TAKE THIS BLESSING FOR GRANTED

THE BLESSING
2004
ACRYLIC ON CANVAS
48 X 36 IN

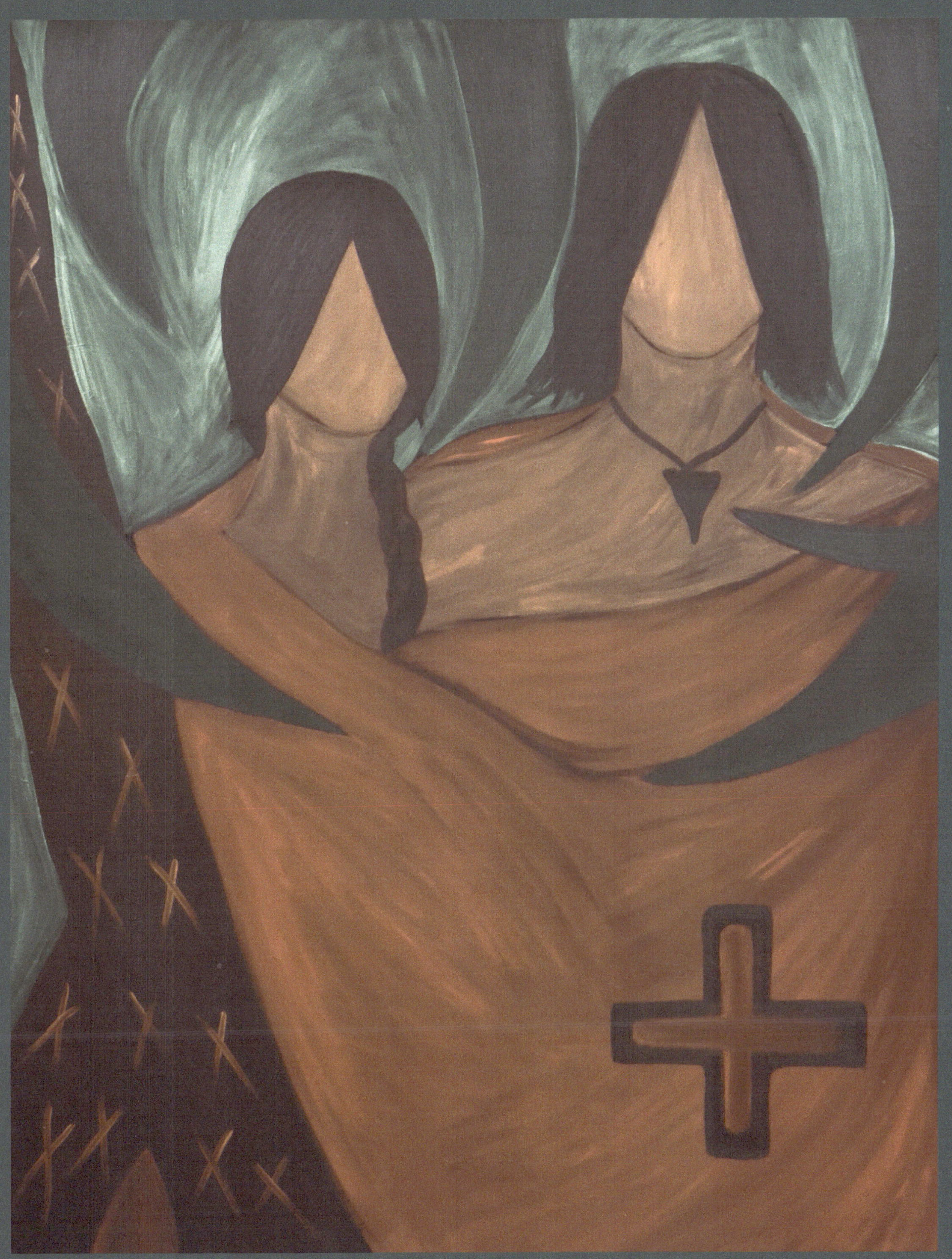

He is known to some as courageous
others call him insane
the only thing they agree upon
is this big wave rider was born to reign

RAIN
2006
ACRYLIC ON CANVAS
48 X 36 IN

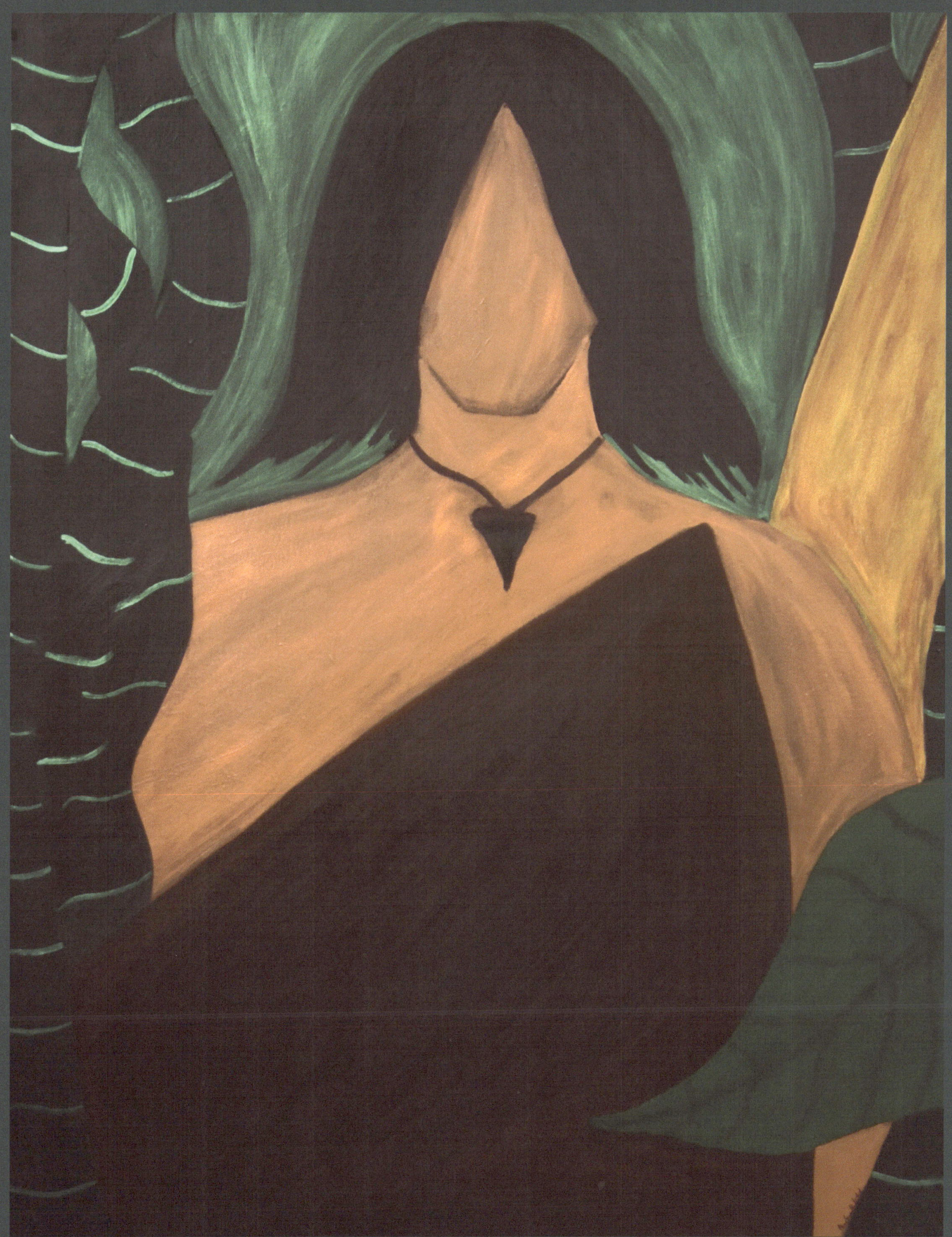

IF WE COULD GO BACK IN TIME
I WOULD BE SQUEEZIN' YOU TIGHT INSTEAD OF THIS LIME

OLIVER
1996
ACRYLIC ON CANVAS
31 X 44 IN

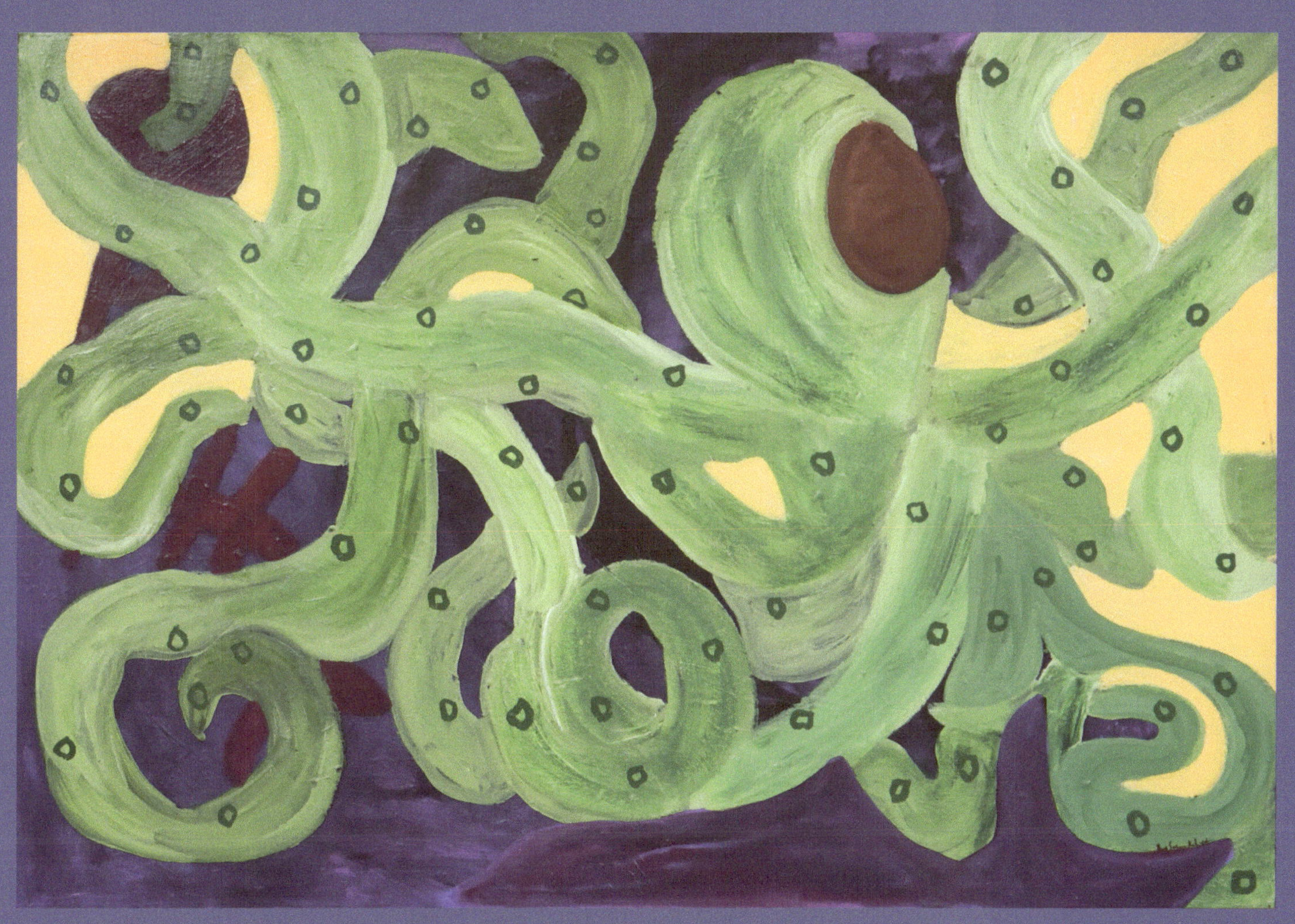

As I sip on various exotic teas
I think of you across the tropical seas

CLAUDIUS
1998
ACRYLIC ON CANVAS
36 X 48 IN
FROM MY CLAW-DIAS SERIES BEGINNING IN 1993

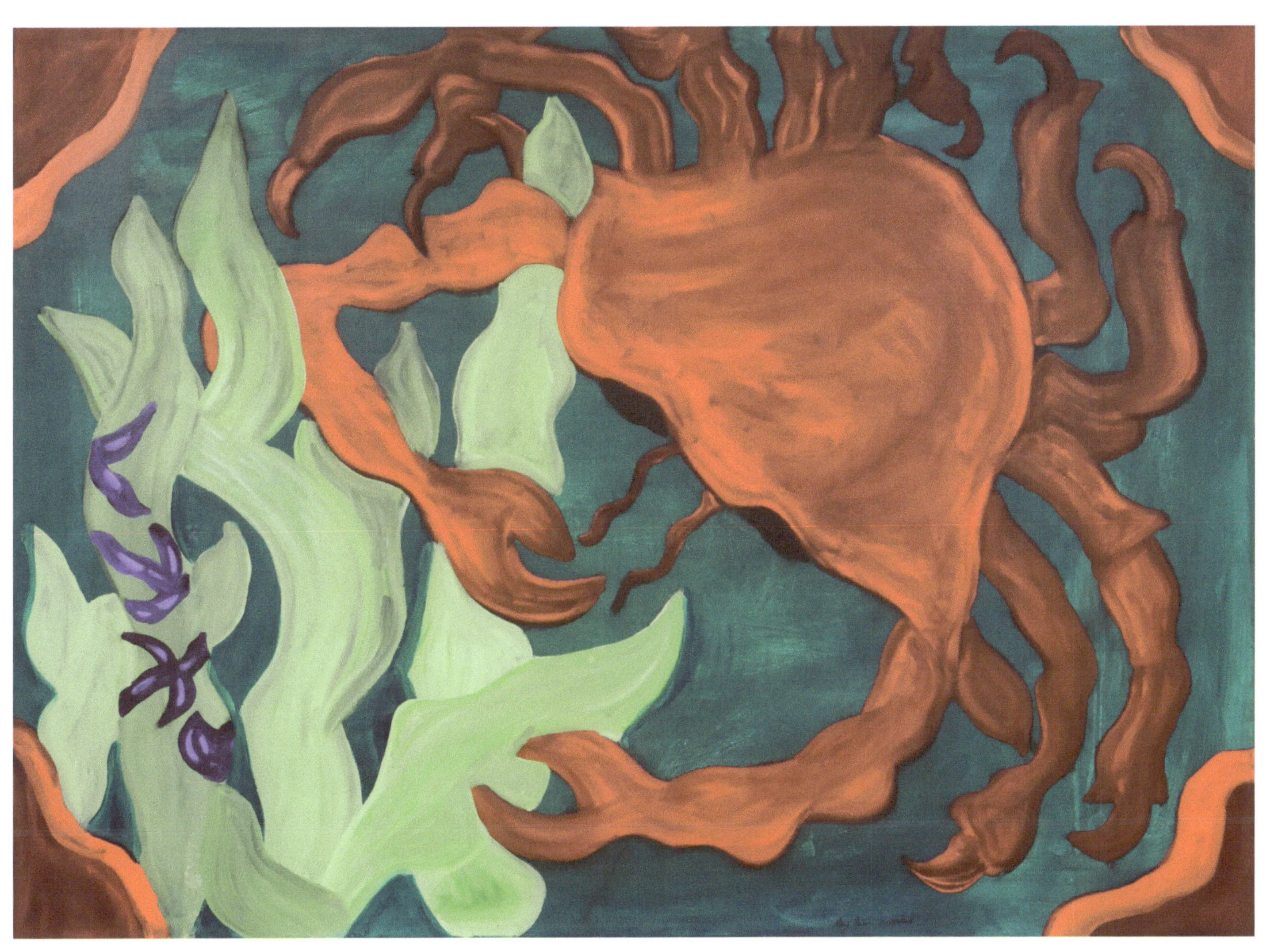

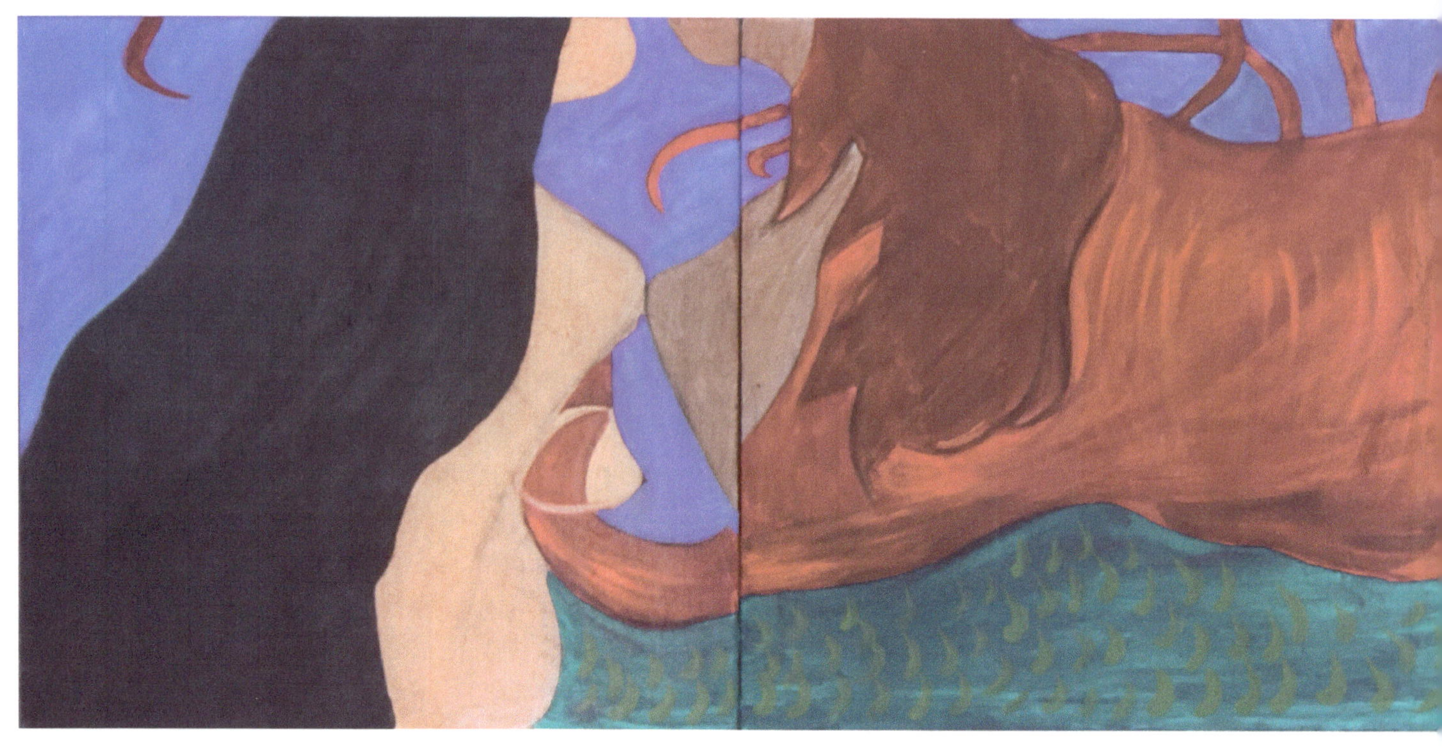

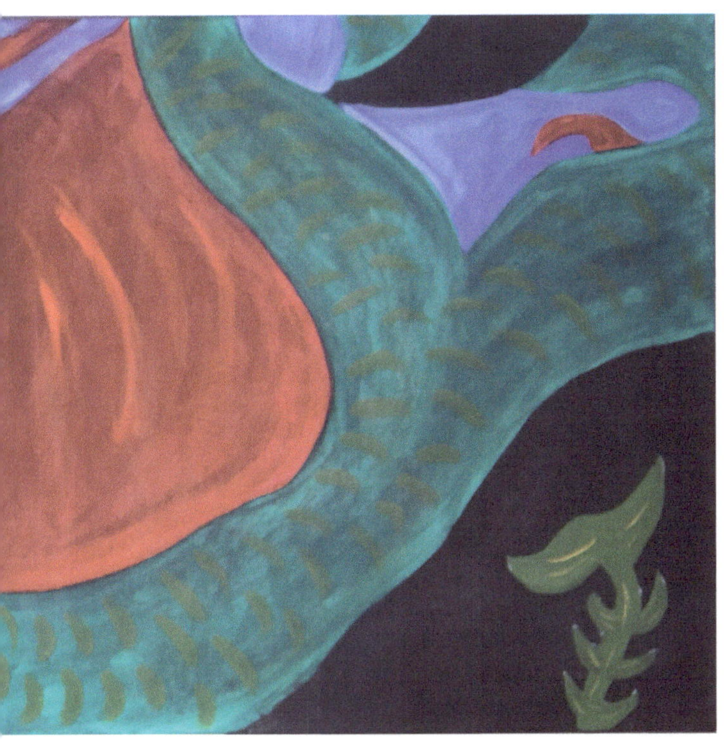

Sea-rinity

2000

Acrylic on canvas

Three 30 x 30 in canvases connected

Overall dimension 30 x 90 in

Eve asked Adam why it was fig leaves they wore
Adam refreshed her and held up the apple core

ISLAND MAN, ICE MAN, ADAM MAN
1991
ACRYLIC ON CANVAS
30 X 30 IN

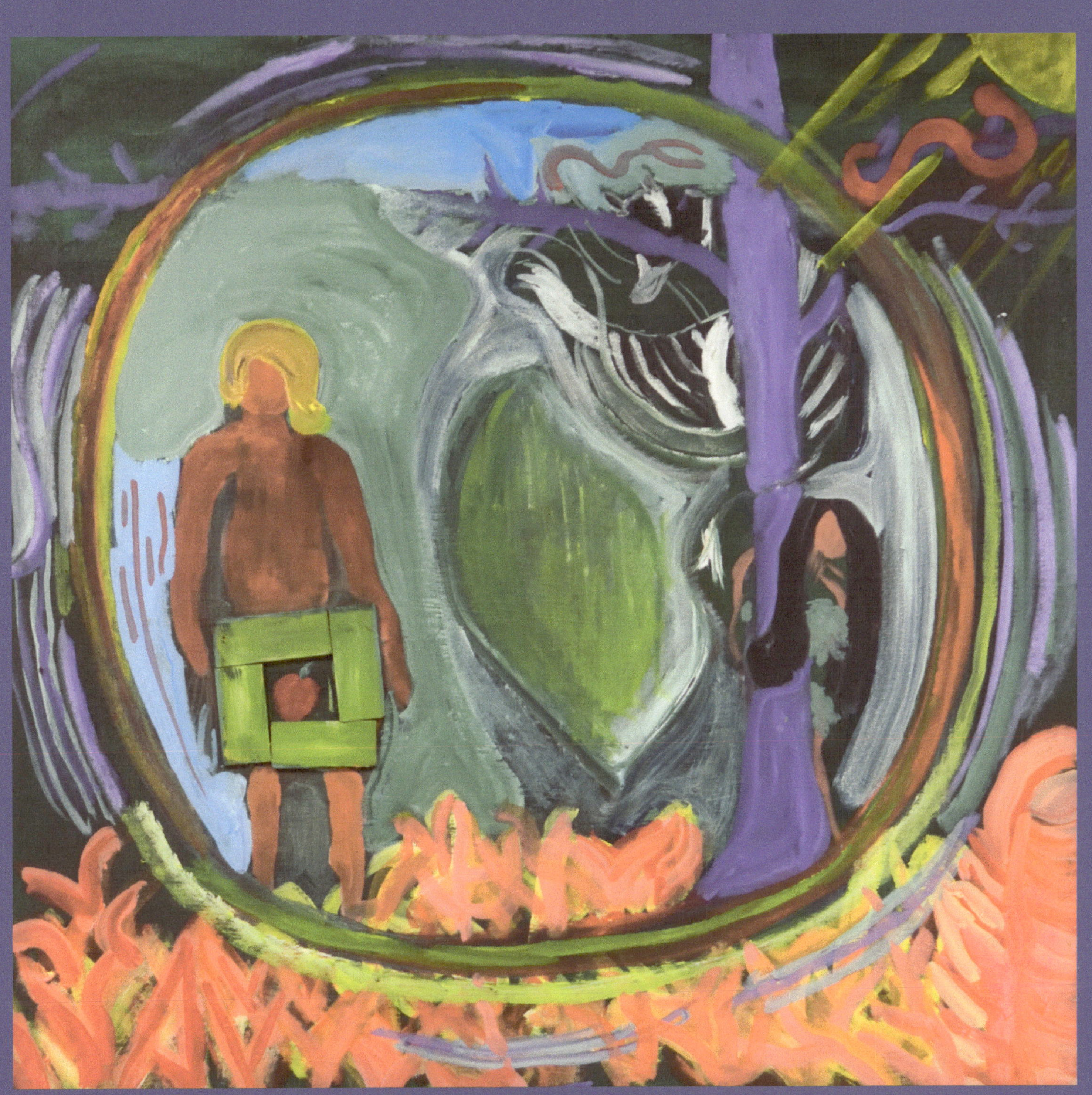

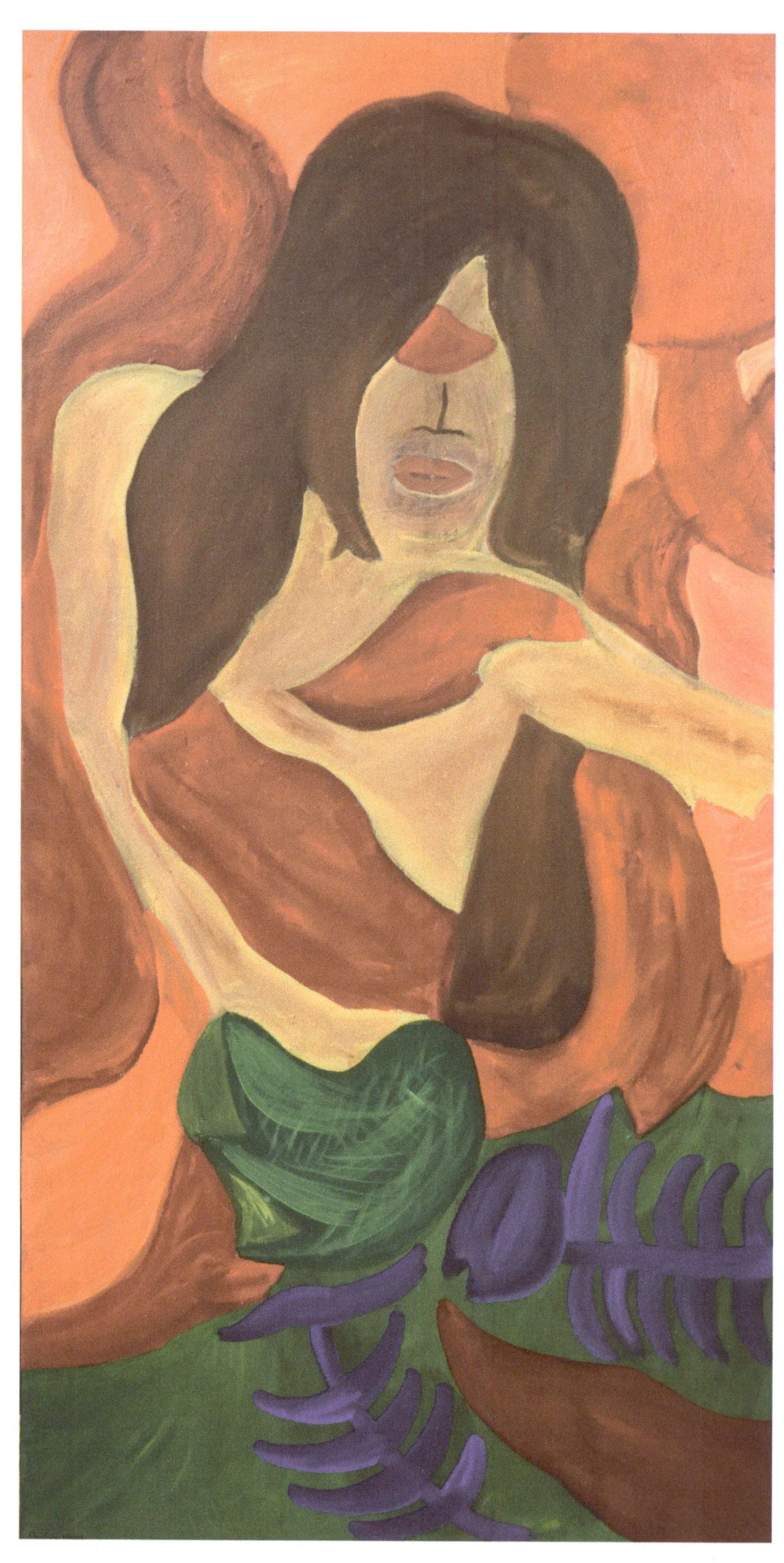

ADD-A-MAN
1995
ACRYLIC ON CANVAS
72 X 36 IN

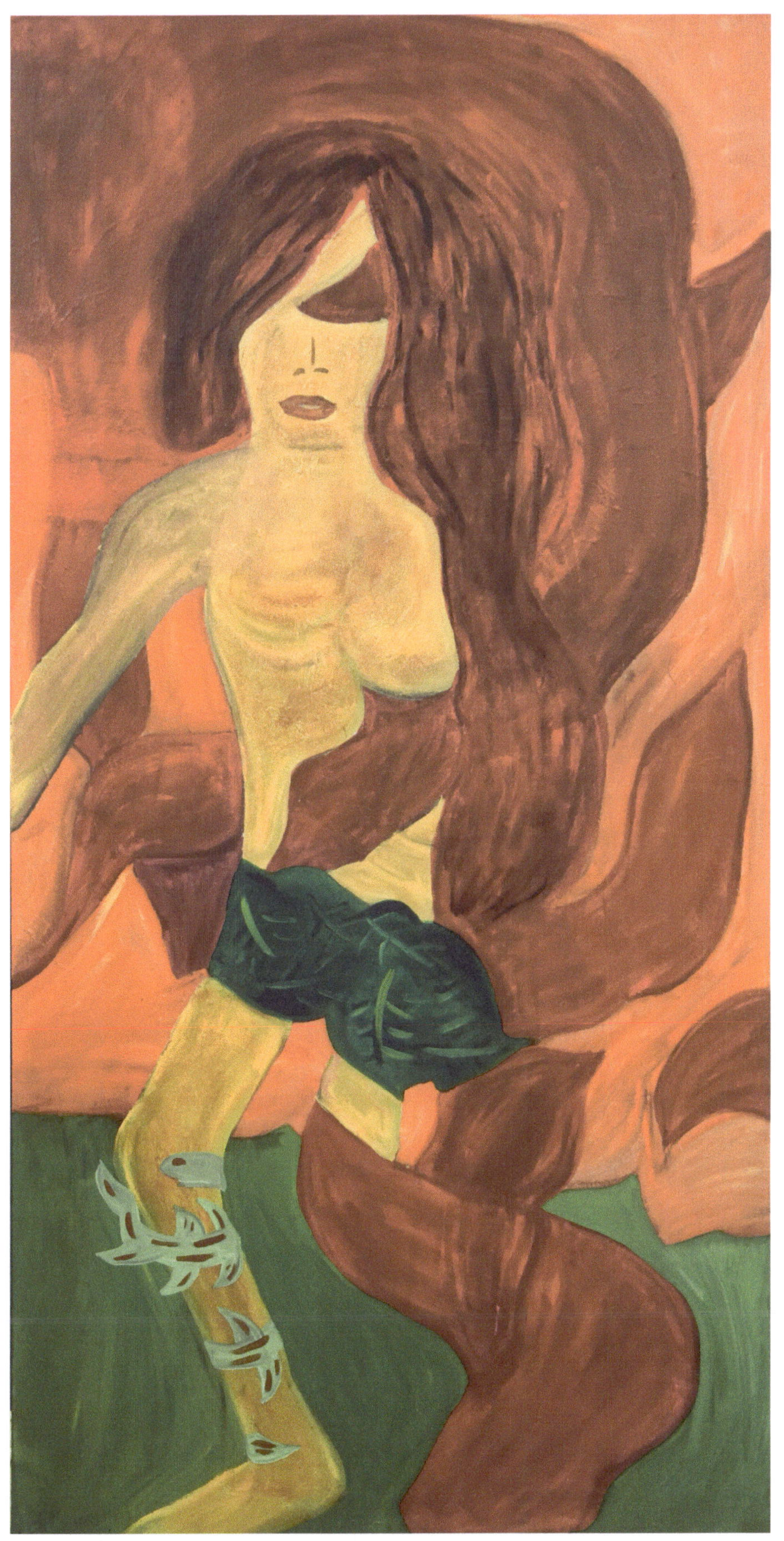

The brontosaur
ate leaves and the
pterodactyl did fly
evolution made it
possible to give our
love a try

Eve-olve
1996
Acrylic on canvas
72 x 36 in

BEAU-HE-ME-N-RIB
ALTHOUGH IT SOUNDS COMPLICATED
IT IS SIMPLE AS CAN BE
THE SAME SINCE THE BEGINNING OF TIME
THE END WE HAVE TO WAIT AND SEE

BEAU-HE-ME-N-RIB
1993
ACRYLIC ON CANVAS
54 X 54 IN

SENIOR STUDIO THESIS EXHIBITION
HUNT-CAVANAGH GALLERY
SPRING 1993

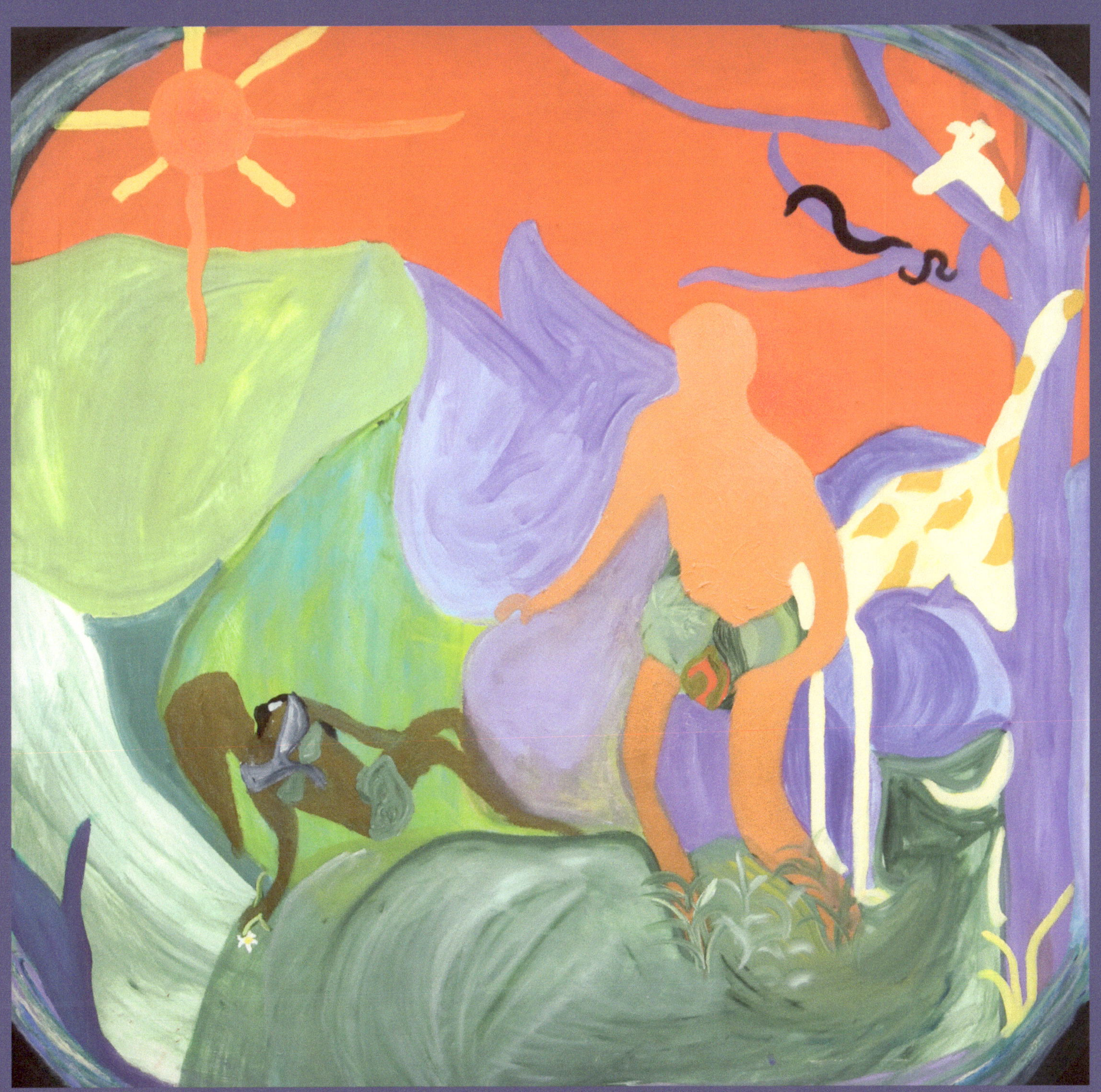

IF YOU WANT TO KNOW THE PENGUIN
WHOSE BELLY SHOWS THE MOST STUFFIN'
ASK THE KRILLS WHO ALWAYS AVOID McGUFFIN

McGUFFIN
2006
ACRYLIC ON CANVAS
48 X 18 IN

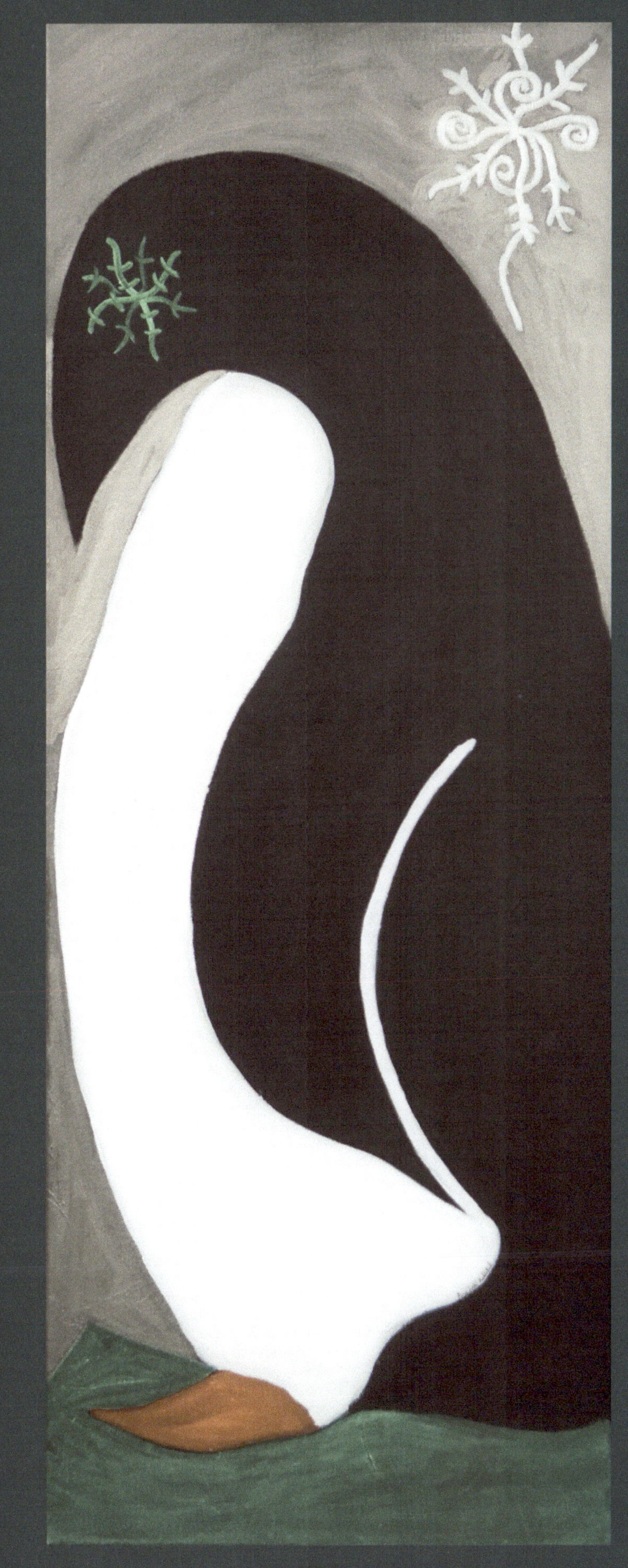

His chiseled face peepin' out of the fur
wiped away all shiverin' and sayin' burrrrrrr

Somewhere Around Kotzebue
1995
Acrylic on canvas
48 x 36 in

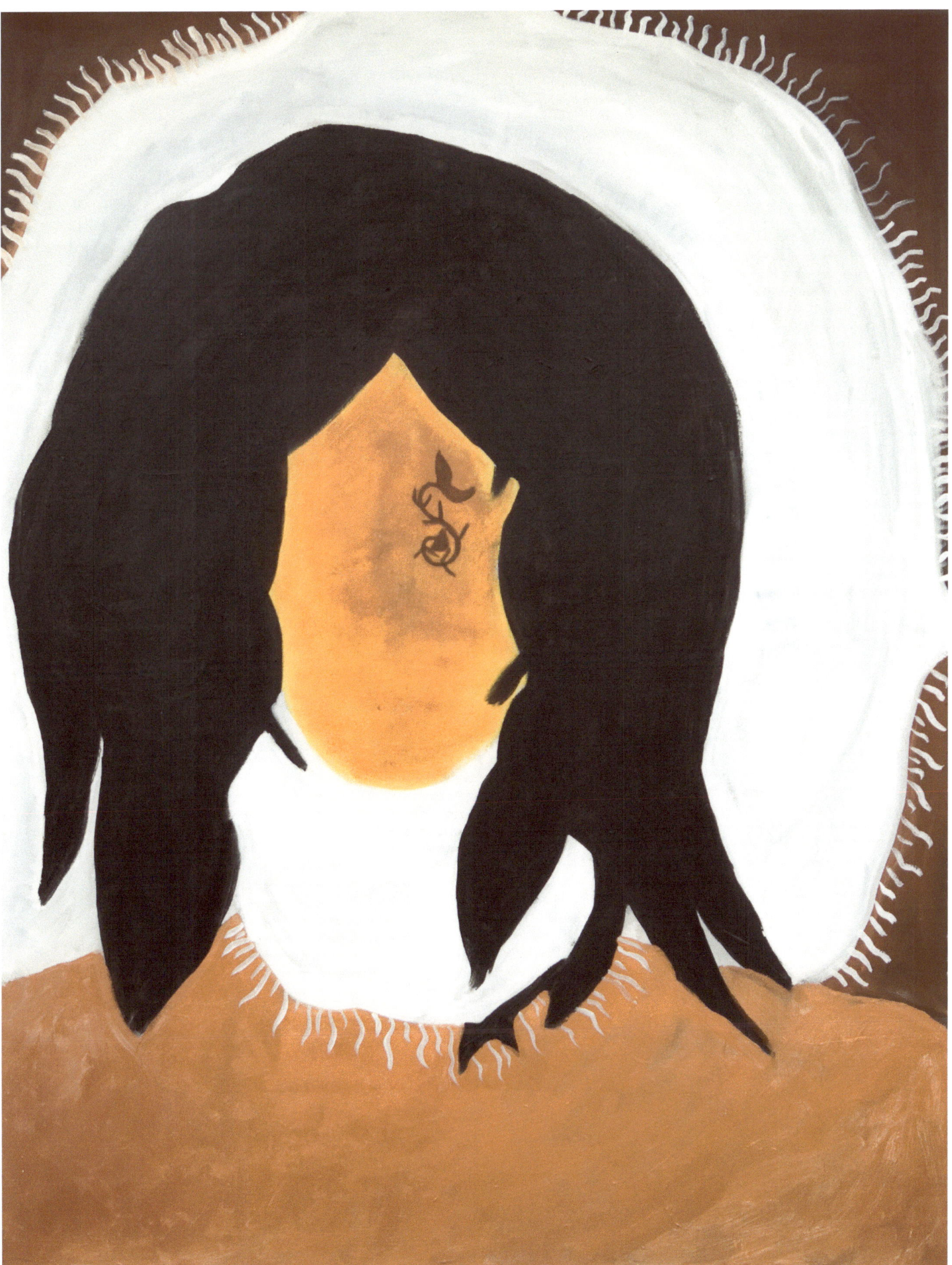

I asked the yellow monkey where my body
could be nourished with food that is fresh
the monkey from Mount Kanchenjunga nodded
and introduced me to a handsome man named Mahesh
then the monkey peeled a banana and offered me a slice
as Mahesh told us the secret to his wisdom
was listening to his own advice
we smiled and then the monkey leaped into the twisted tree
suddenly realizing there was no need for three

THE MONKEY FROM MOUNT KANCHENJUNGA
2003
ACRYLIC ON CANVAS
49 X 42 IN

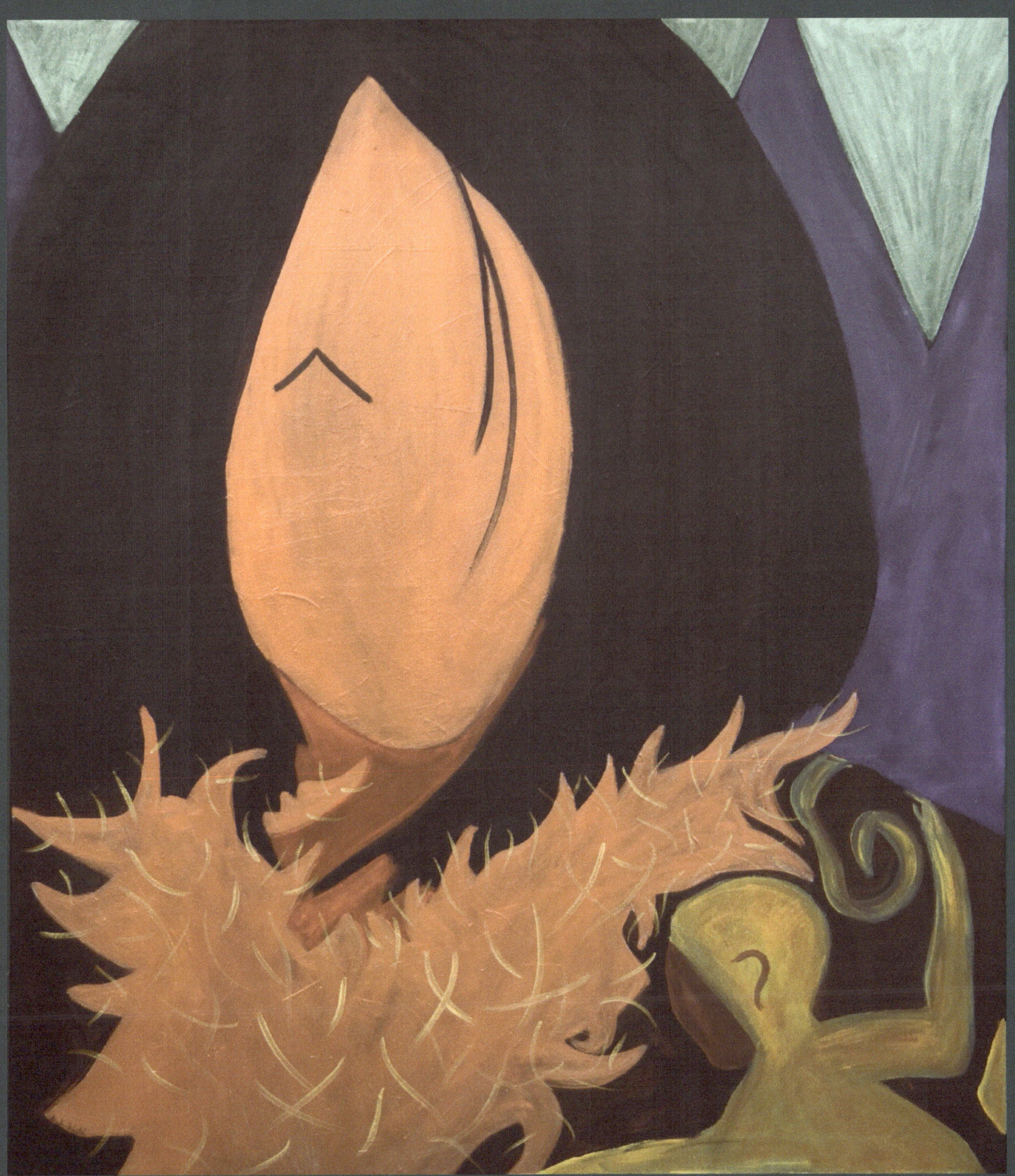

FAREWELL TO SUN SALUTATIONS
NO MORE INHALING AND EXHALING MONITORED BY SOME
SELF PROCLAIMED GURU
I WAS NOW SAFE AMONGST THE JAGGED WALL OF ICE
UNDER A LIGHT OF COPPER HUE
PATH OF FISHBONES SCATTERED ON THE FRAGILE GROUND
AT THE END
HIS EYE HELD THE LONG AWAITED ANSWER
AND I KNEW IT WAS PROFOUND
IT TURNED OUT NEITHER ONE OF US SPOKE
THERE WAS NO NEED
AS THE JAGGED WALL OF ICE BROKE

JAGGED ICE
2008
ACRYLIC ON CANVAS
60 X 48 IN

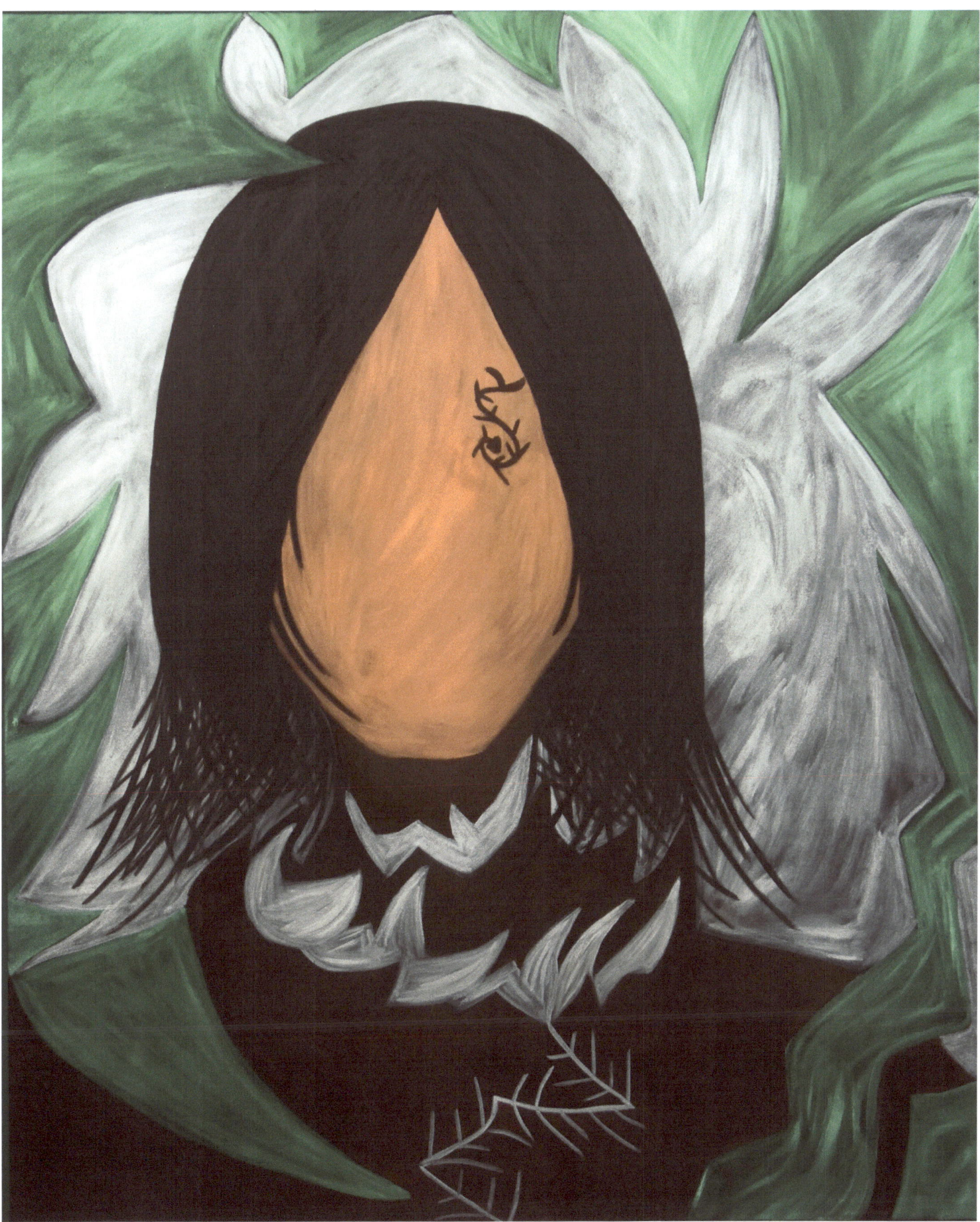

SILENCE
ONCE MORE
THE CANOE DRAWS NEAR
NOCTURNAL MEETING WITH THE PRAYING MANTIS
TELEPATHIC WISDOM
IT ALL BECOMES CLEAR
I SUDDENLY GRASP THE DELICATE BRANCH NEARBY
AN ABUNDANCE OF STARS
THE VISUAL LINGUISTICS OF THE SKY
THE PRAYING MANTIS CAREFULLY OBSERVING
THE SURROUNDING SPACE
IN THE USUAL POSITION OF SAYING GRACE
SILENCE
THIS MIDNIGHT MOMENT I SAVE
THE HYPNOTIZING STARS
THE VISION OF THE BRAVE

SILENCE
1991
OIL AND ACRYLIC ON CANVAS
20 X 16 IN

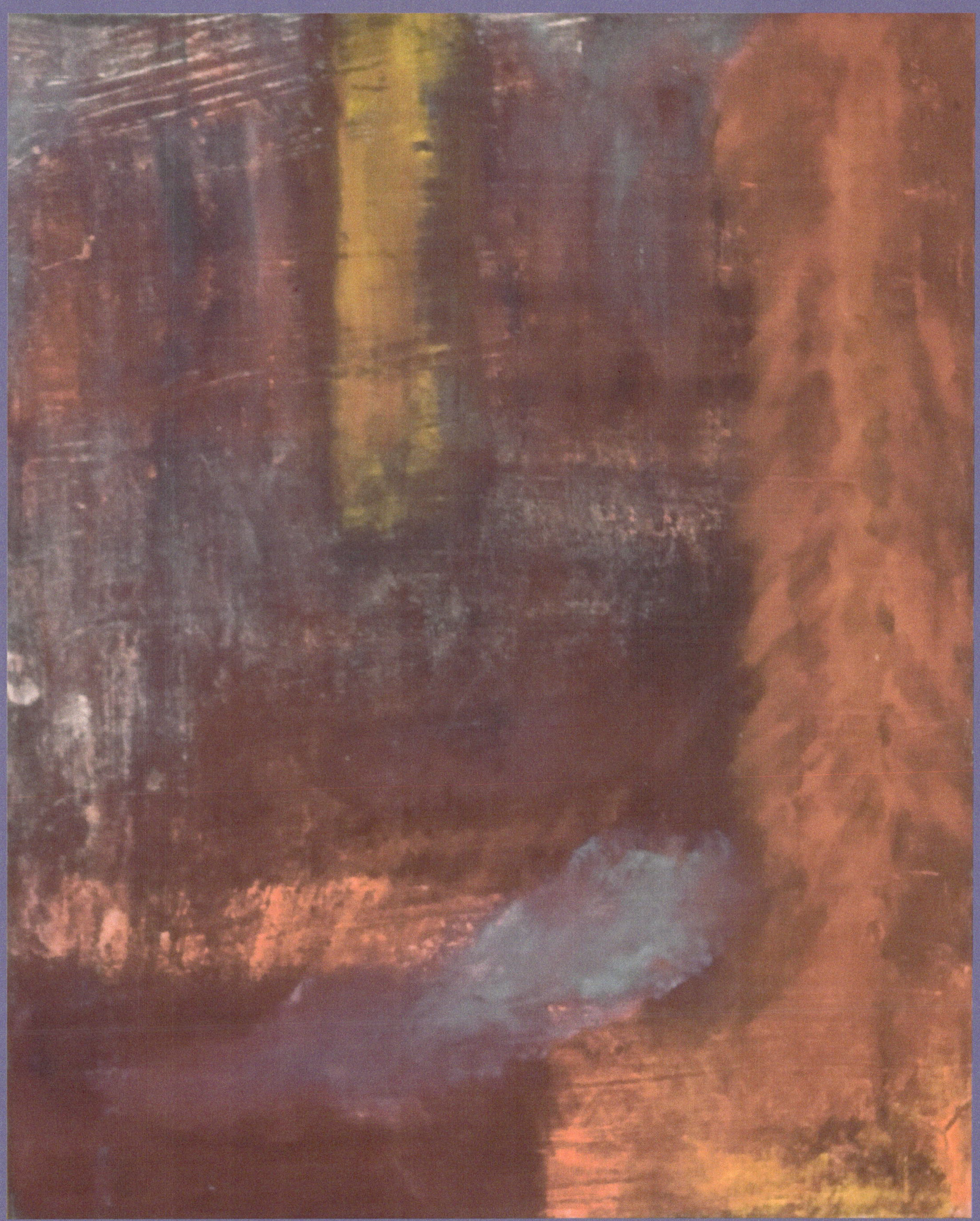

My lungs invite in the dry desert air
your raspy whisper allows me to know you are still there
darkness appeared over the red rocks sooner than expected
for you though it was no surprise
my heart beats like the drum in the distance
the same heart that has become my eyes

Whisper
1987
Acrylic on canvas
30 x 24 in

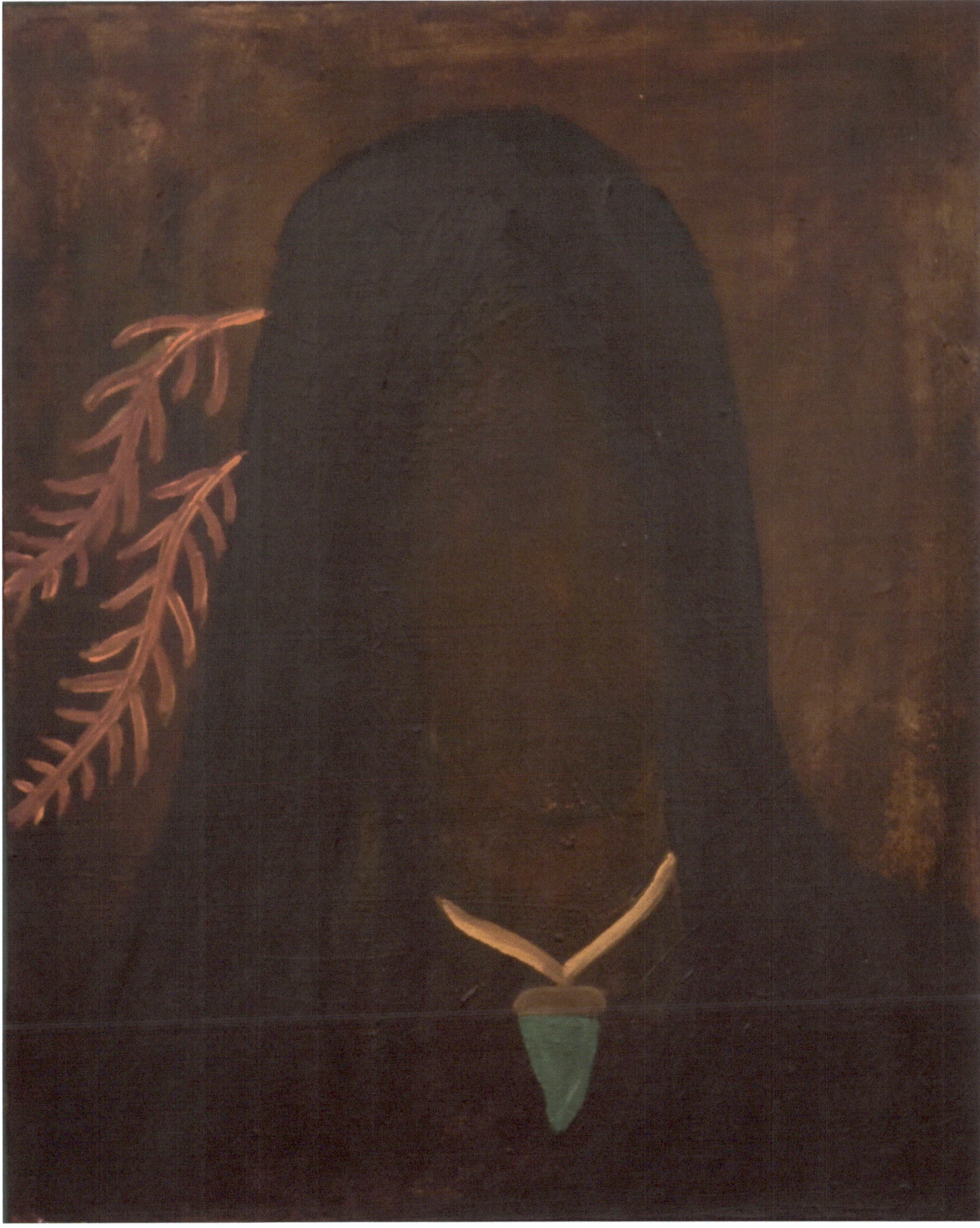

CONTINUE TO STING
AND WHEN YOU FIND ME
PLEASE
I ASK
DO NOT RESUSCITATE
NO LECTURES
THAT YOU STILL NEED ME
AND HOW THE ANGELS CAN WAIT

SCORPIO
2001
ACRYLIC ON CANVAS
47 X 40 IN

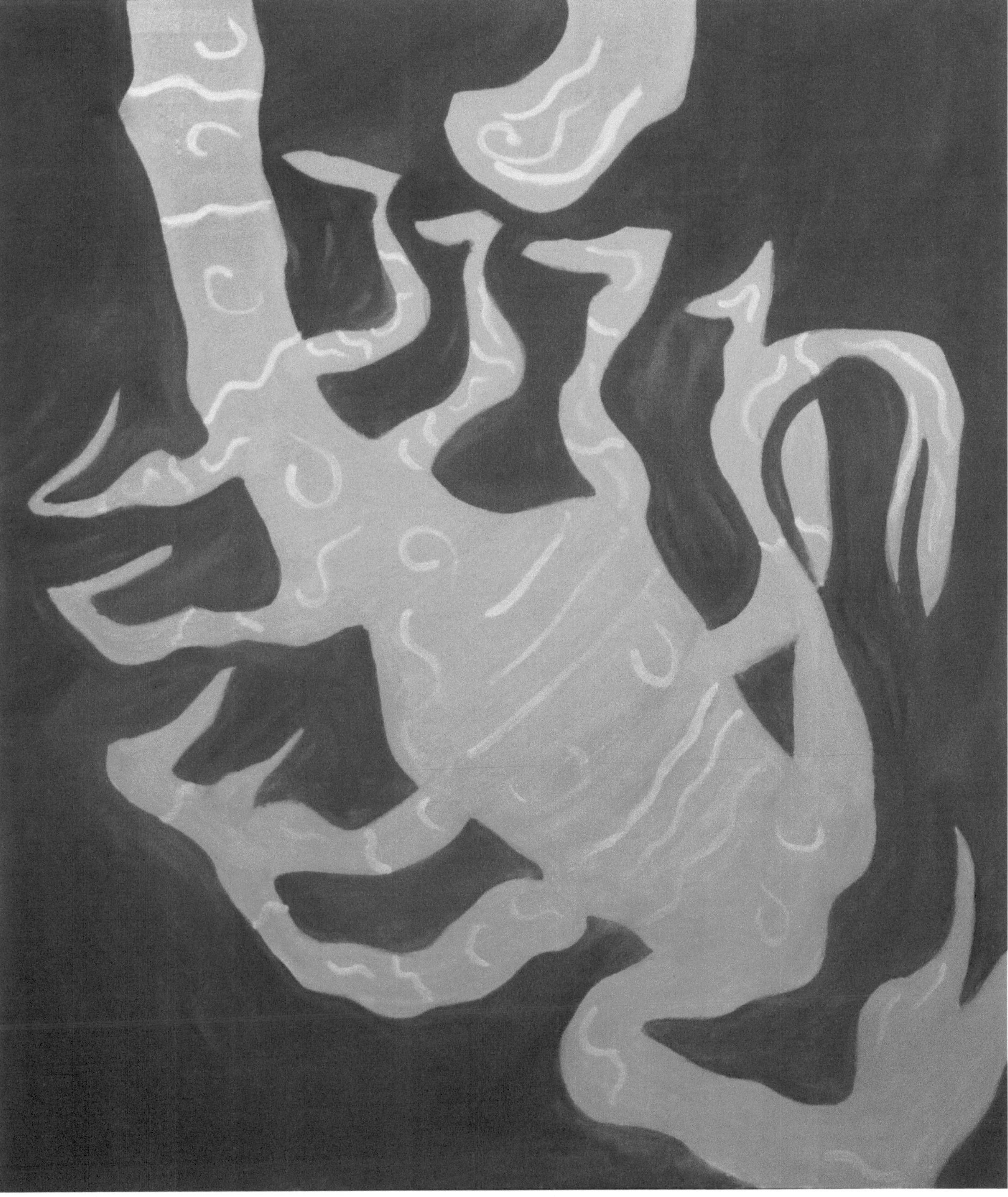

RUSHING THROUGH HIS VEINS
LIKE A RAPID FLOOD
IS THE EVER FLOW OF HIS CHEROKEE BLOOD
HE FOCUSES INTENTLY
THE RIVER AHEAD
THE SACRIFICE OF HIS ANCESTORS
THE ONES THAT HAVE BLED

BYE-SUN
1993
ACRYLIC ON CANVAS
42 X 42 IN

SENIOR STUDIO THESIS EXHIBITION
HUNT-CAVANAGH GALLERY
SPRING 1993

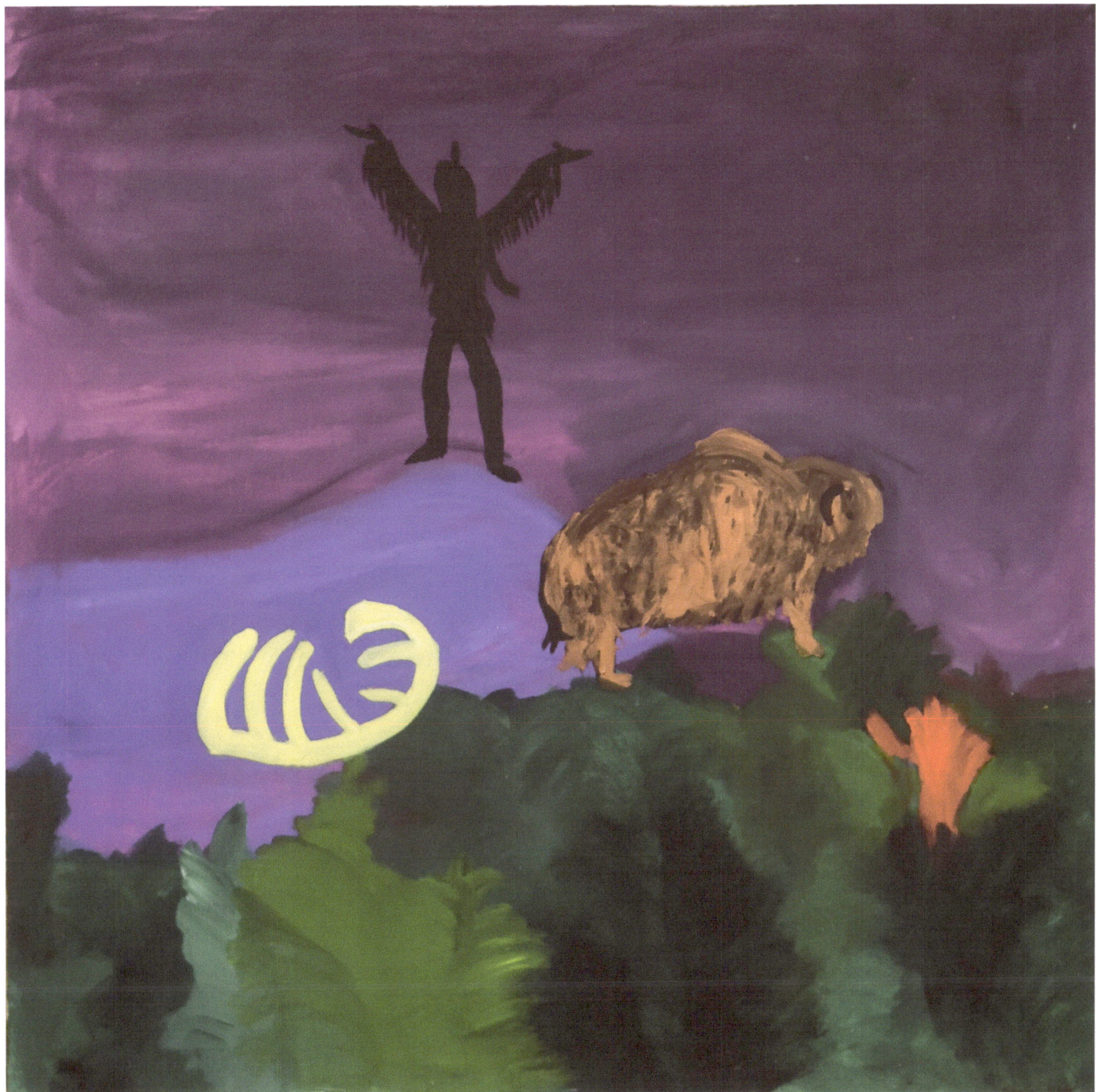

THE JADED DESERT ONCE AGAIN DOES REVIVE
IT IS THE SPIRIT OF THE TRIBE THAT ALLOWS IT TO SURVIVE

JADED REVIVAL
1992
ACRYLIC ON CANVAS
42 X 36 IN

SENIOR STUDIO THESIS EXHIBITION
HUNT-CAVANAGH GALLERY
SPRING 1993

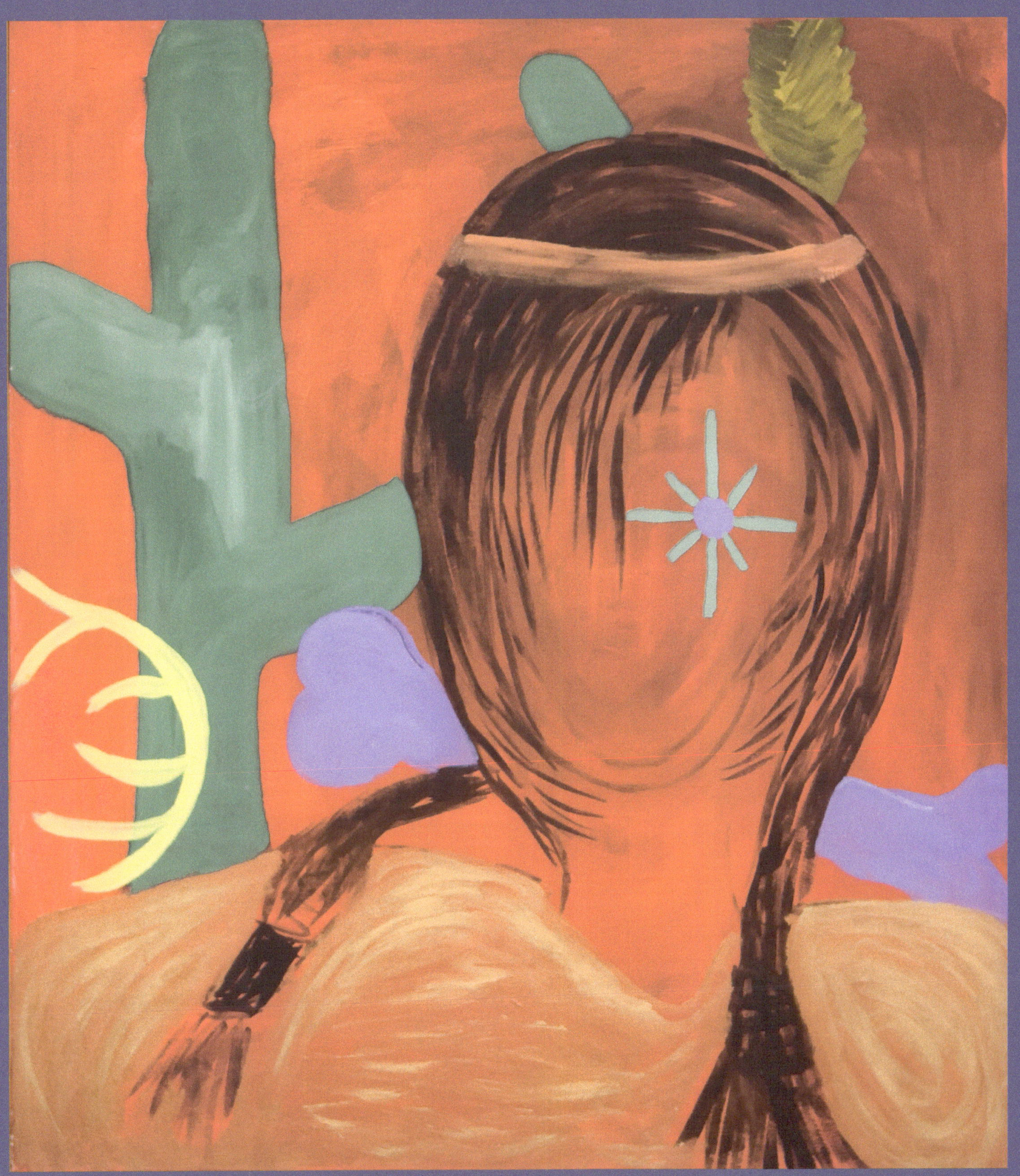

BONE OF THE BUFFALO
CAUGHT OUT OF THE CORNER OF HIS EYE
HIS FEATHERS ILLUMINATE UNDER THE DEEP PURPLE SKY
HE WAITS STILL
THE TREE IS THE ONLY THING IN SIGHT
IT HAS BEEN THAT WAY SINCE THE WILD GOOSE TOOK FLIGHT
HIS SKIN
THE SHADE OF EARTH'S CLAY
TIME LOST
DAY AFTER DAY
WONDERING WHY HE IS ALONE
AS HE ONCE MORE STARES AT THE BUFFALO BONE

BONE OF THE BUFFALO
2002
ACRYLIC ON CANVAS
42 X 36 IN

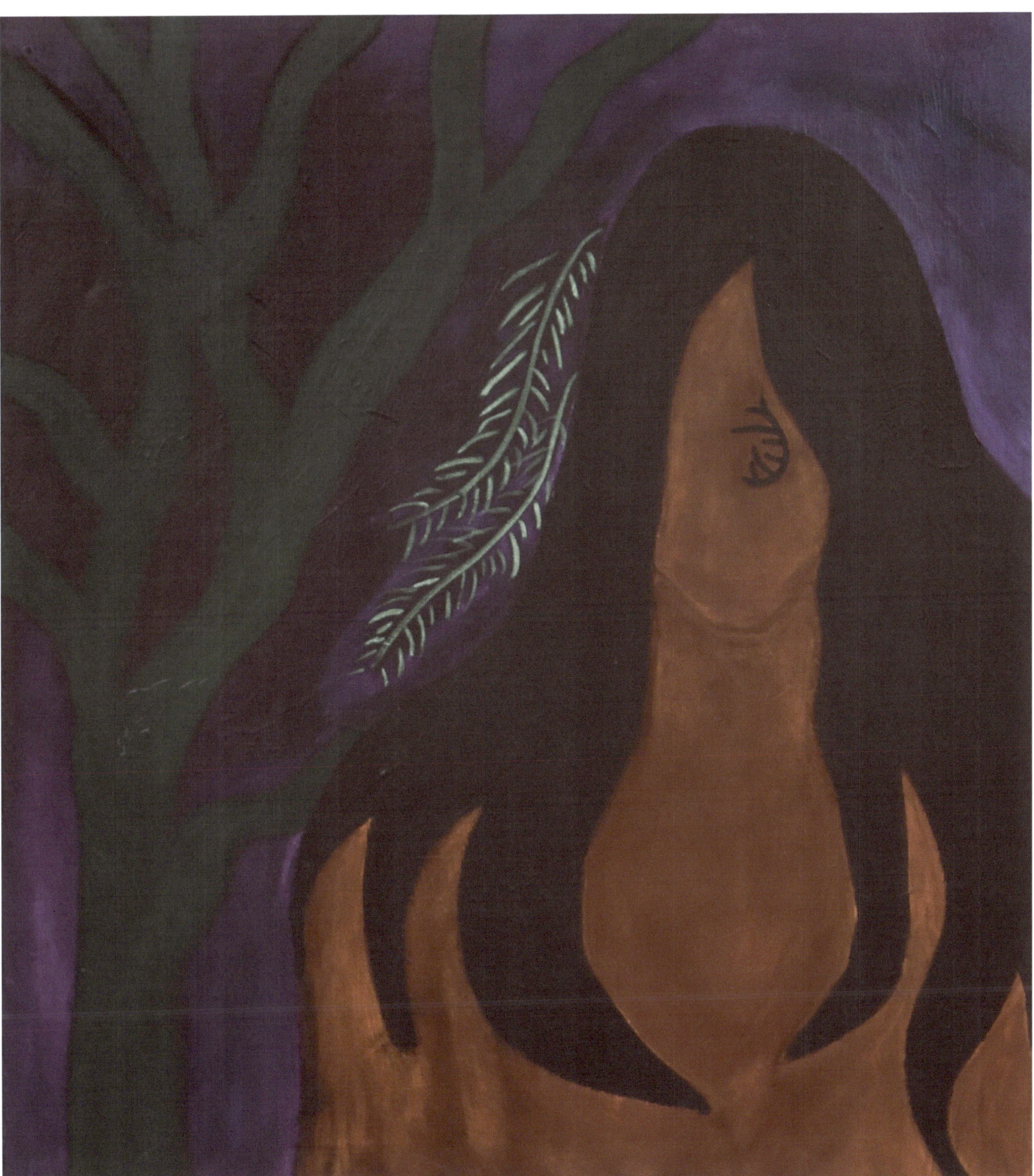

Cactus
evident of your loyalty
yet
your piercing needles
cause us to keep our distance
almost how
love
can be
for instance

CREED
2005
ACRYLIC ON CANVAS
48 X 36 IN

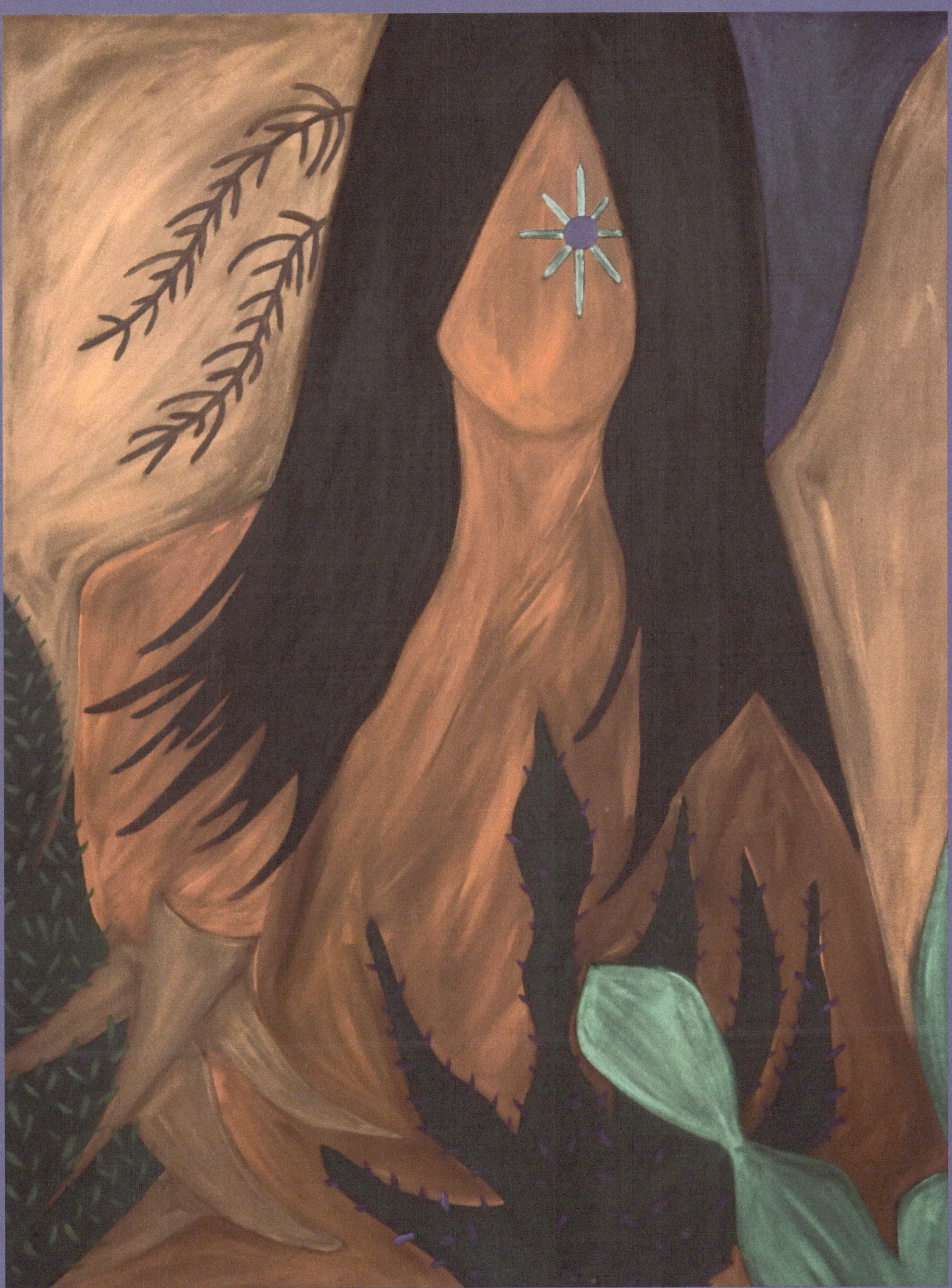

Trees saturated with spanish moss
arrow awaits
in the paths that cross

Arrow
2002
Acrylic on canvas
48 x 46 in

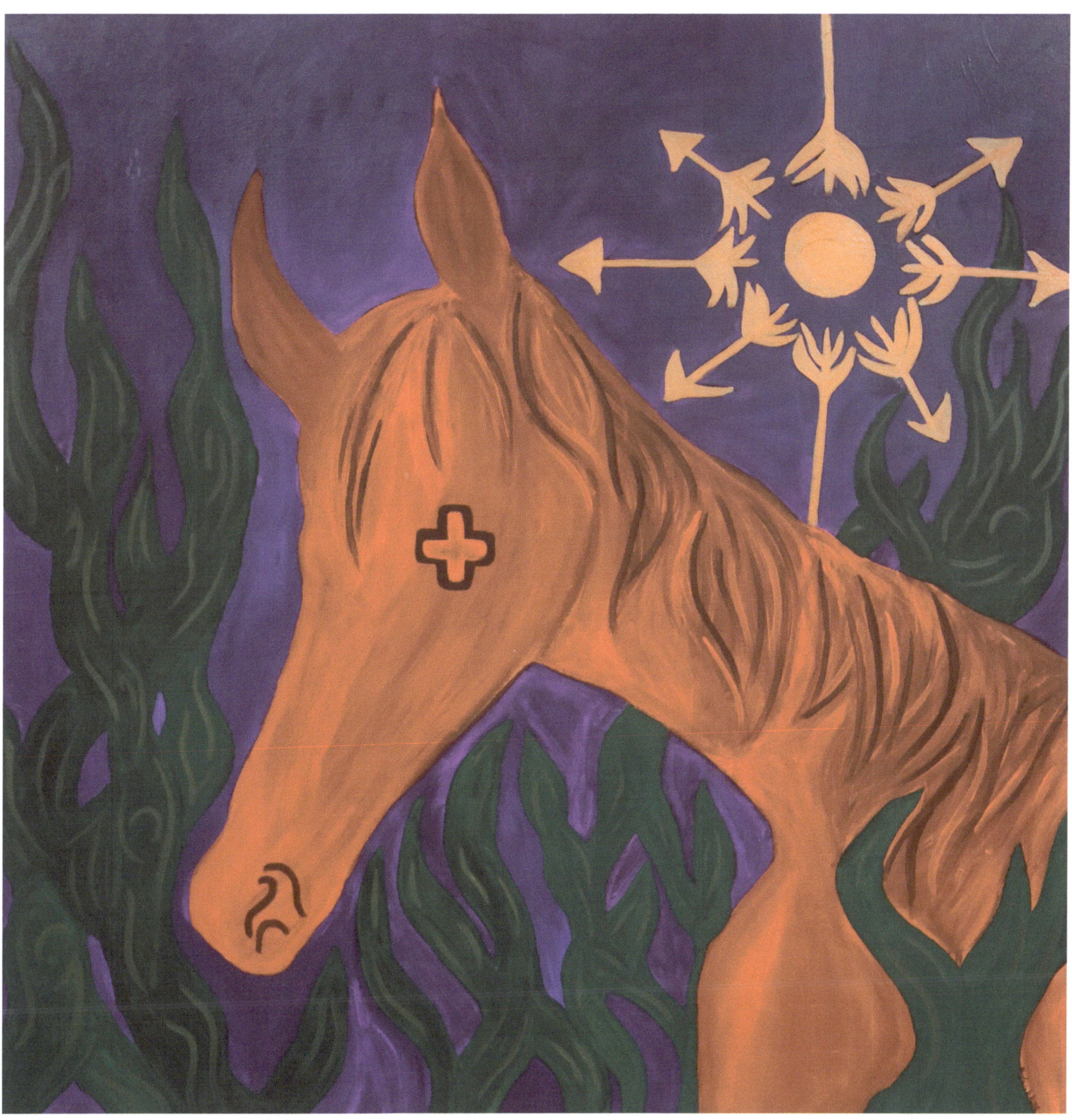

BEHIND THE GREEN BLADE OF GRASS
AHEAD OF HIS YOUNG YEARS
THE WARRIOR
MOTIONLESS
THE ONE WHO HAS NO FEARS
BEHIND THE THICK BLADE OF GRASS
AHEAD OF ALL THE REST
THE WARRIOR
CONFIRMS
HE IS STILL KNOWN AS THE BEST

187 FULL MOONS
2007
ACRYLIC ON CANVAS
60 X 48 IN

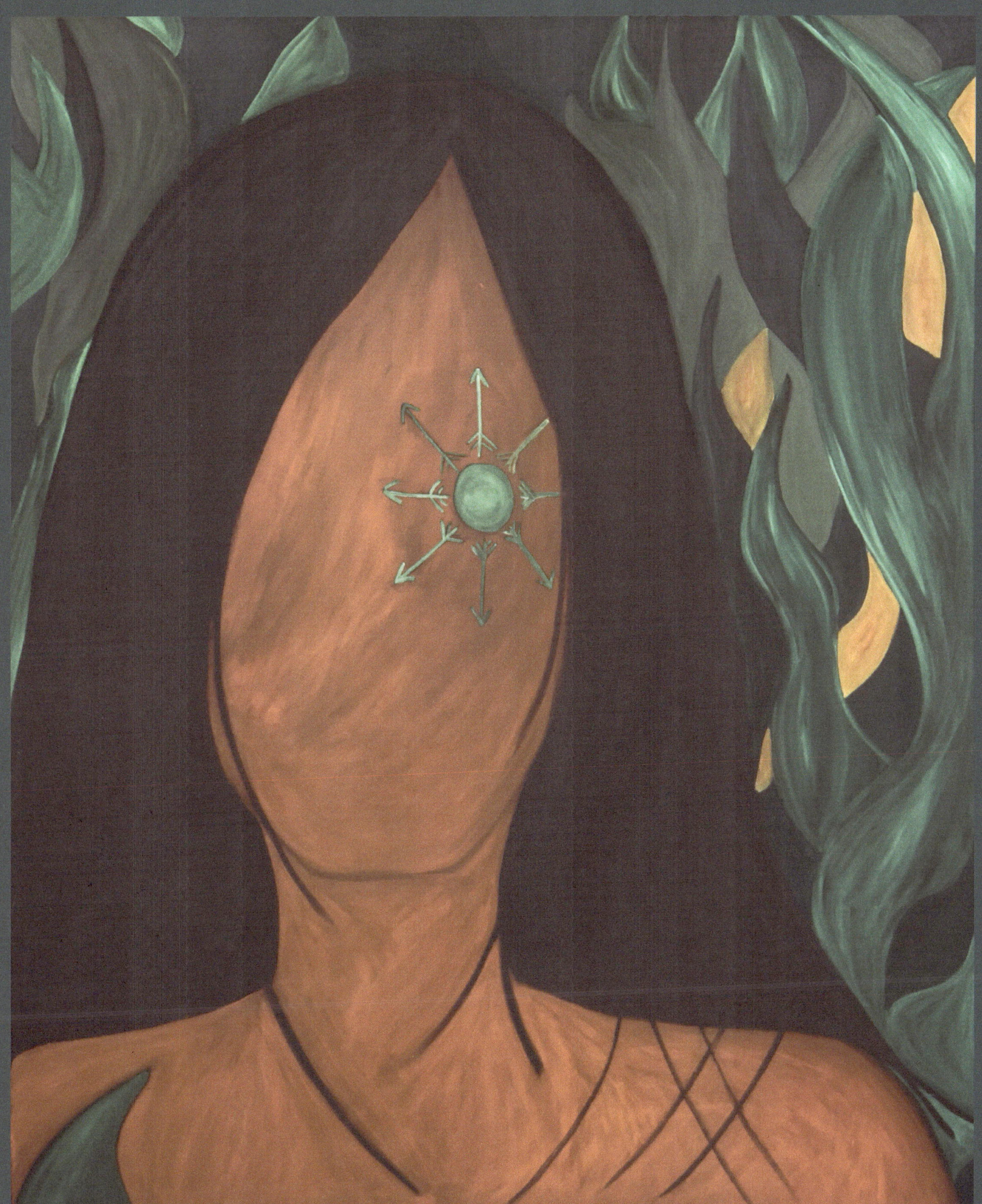

BAMBOO EMBRACES ALL AROUND
IN THE DISTANCE
MUD SINKS INTO THE HALLOW GROUND
ASIAN ANGEL WONDERS IF I AM AWARE
THAT HE IS WATCHING
WHILE MY HEART SENDS TO HEAVEN
MY PRAYER

PRAYER
2004
ACRYLIC ON CANVAS
48 X 36 IN

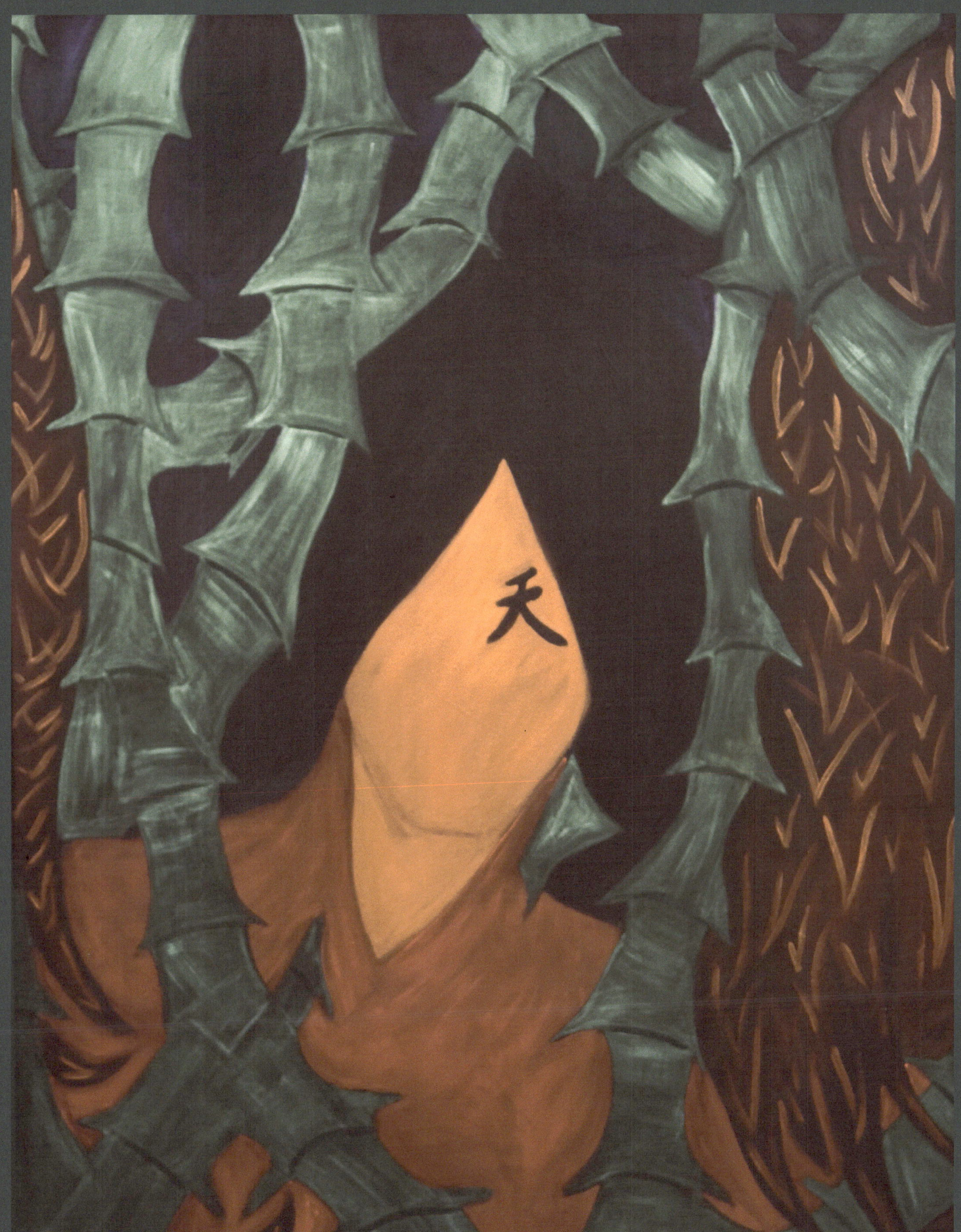
天

Blooms
the promise of spring
telepathy
the message
my friend from Beijing

BAY-JING
2003
ACRYLIC ON CANVAS
47 X 15 IN

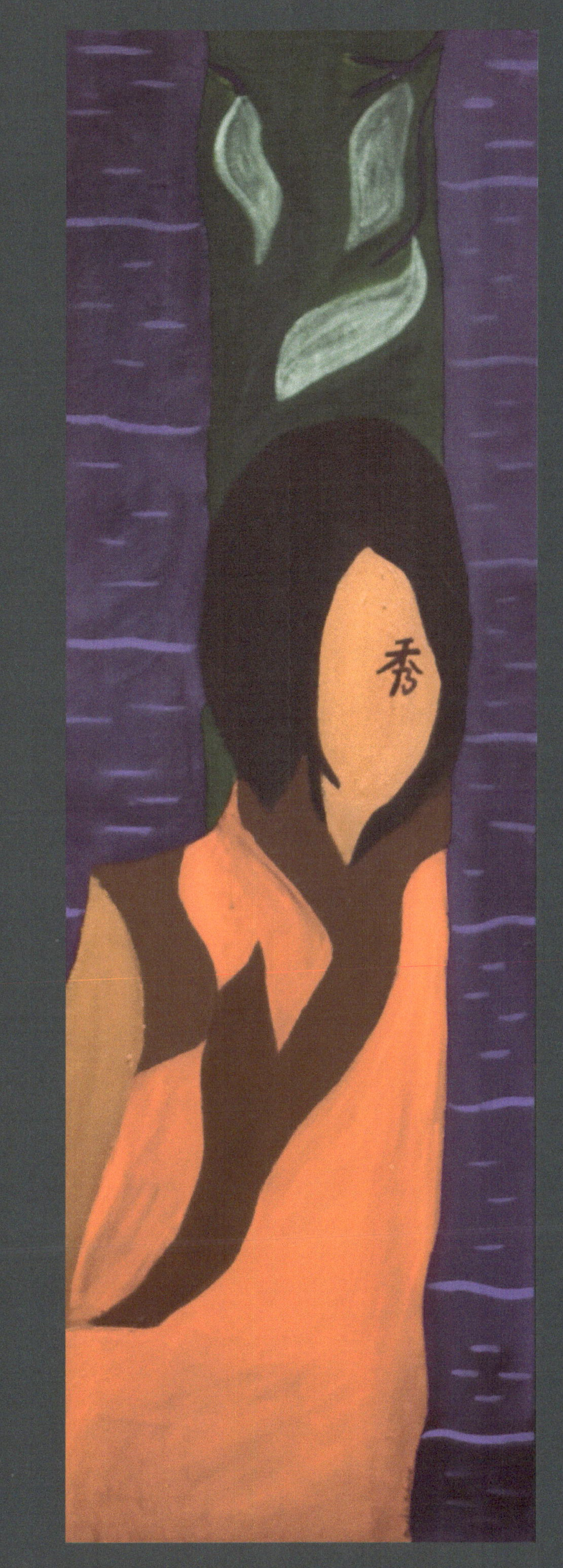
秀

MEN IN PLAID WITH BAGPIPES IN HAND
A FOGGY CHILL CROSSES OVER SCOTLAND
THE LOCH NESS MYSTERY AND STORIES OF CASTLES BUILT
I THINK OF IT ALL
SURROUNDED IN THE WEED OF THE KILT

WEED OF THE KILT
1996
ACRYLIC ON CANVAS
30 X 30 IN

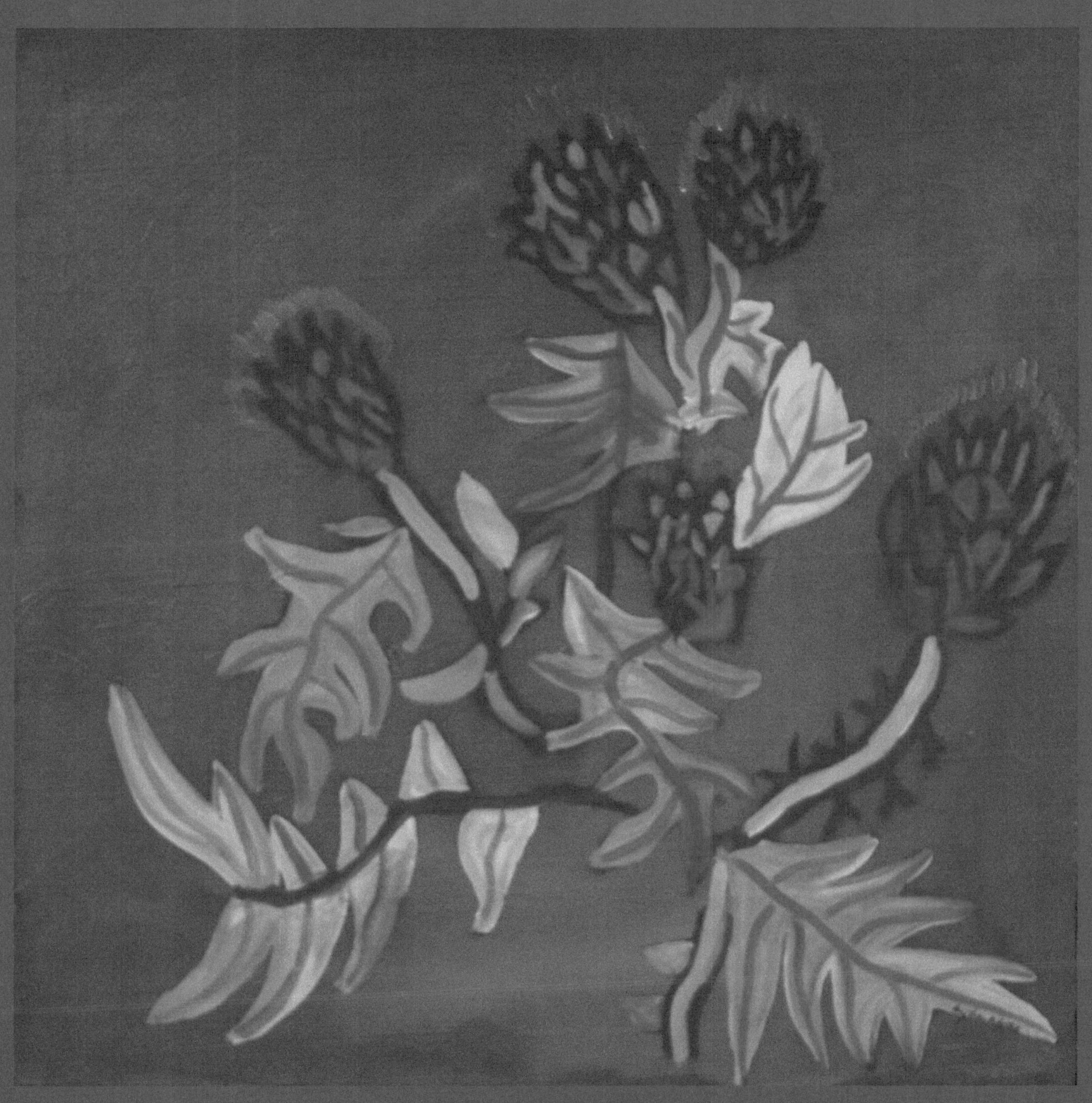

DO YOU REMEMBER THE HAGGIS?
OR THE THISTLE BENEATH THE WALL OF STONE?
DO YOU REMEMBER THE PAST?
AND HOW ITS FUTURE HAS FLOWN

DO YOU REMEMBER THE HAGGIS?
1993
ACRYLIC ON CANVAS
60 X 10 IN SET OF TWO

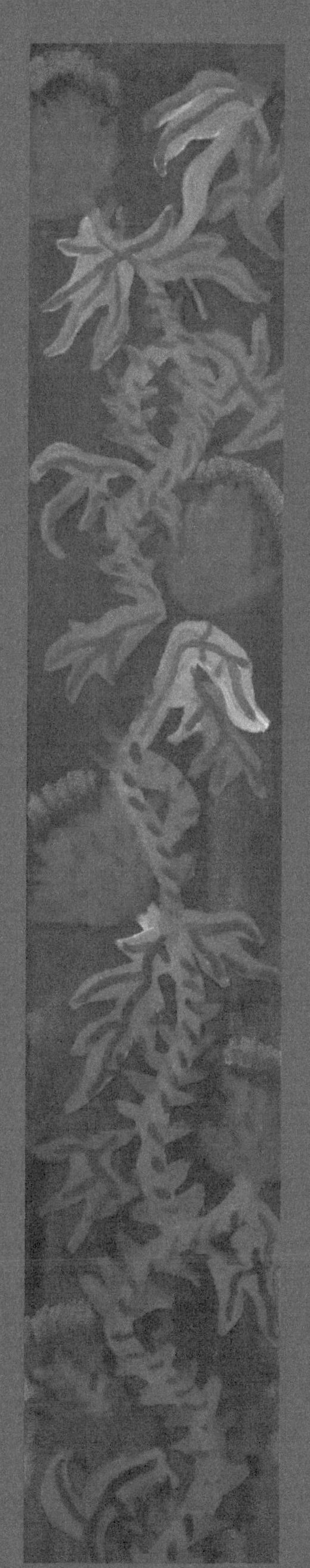
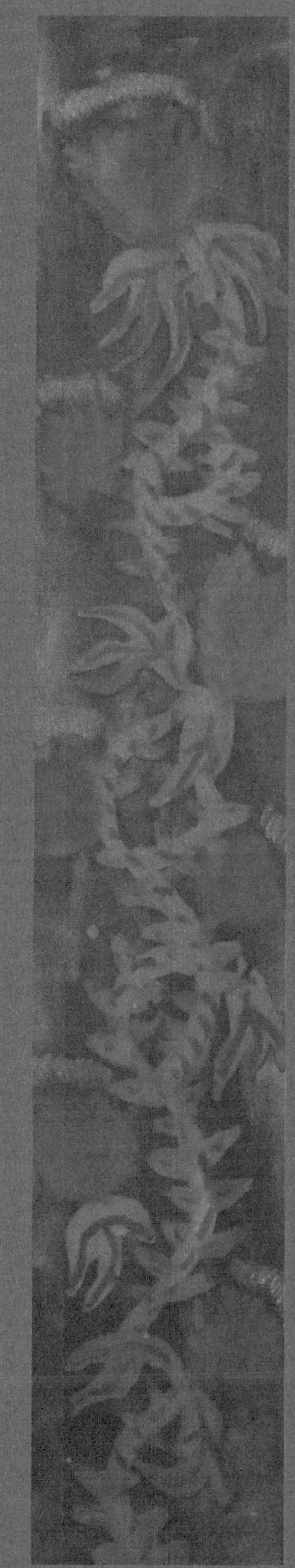

DANDELIONS DOMINATE THE OPEN FIELD
VINTAGE SUITCASE CLOSE TO ME
I SIT
BUT I DO NOT SLEEP
I HAVE NO TIME TO BE COUNTING SHEEP
I WAIT
FOR WHAT? THEY ASK
I TELL THEM I ALREADY HAVE A RIDE
I AM ANXIOUS TO SEE WHAT IS ON THE OTHER SIDE

POLO OUT OF THIS WORLD
1996
ACRYLIC ON CANVAS
24 X 20 IN

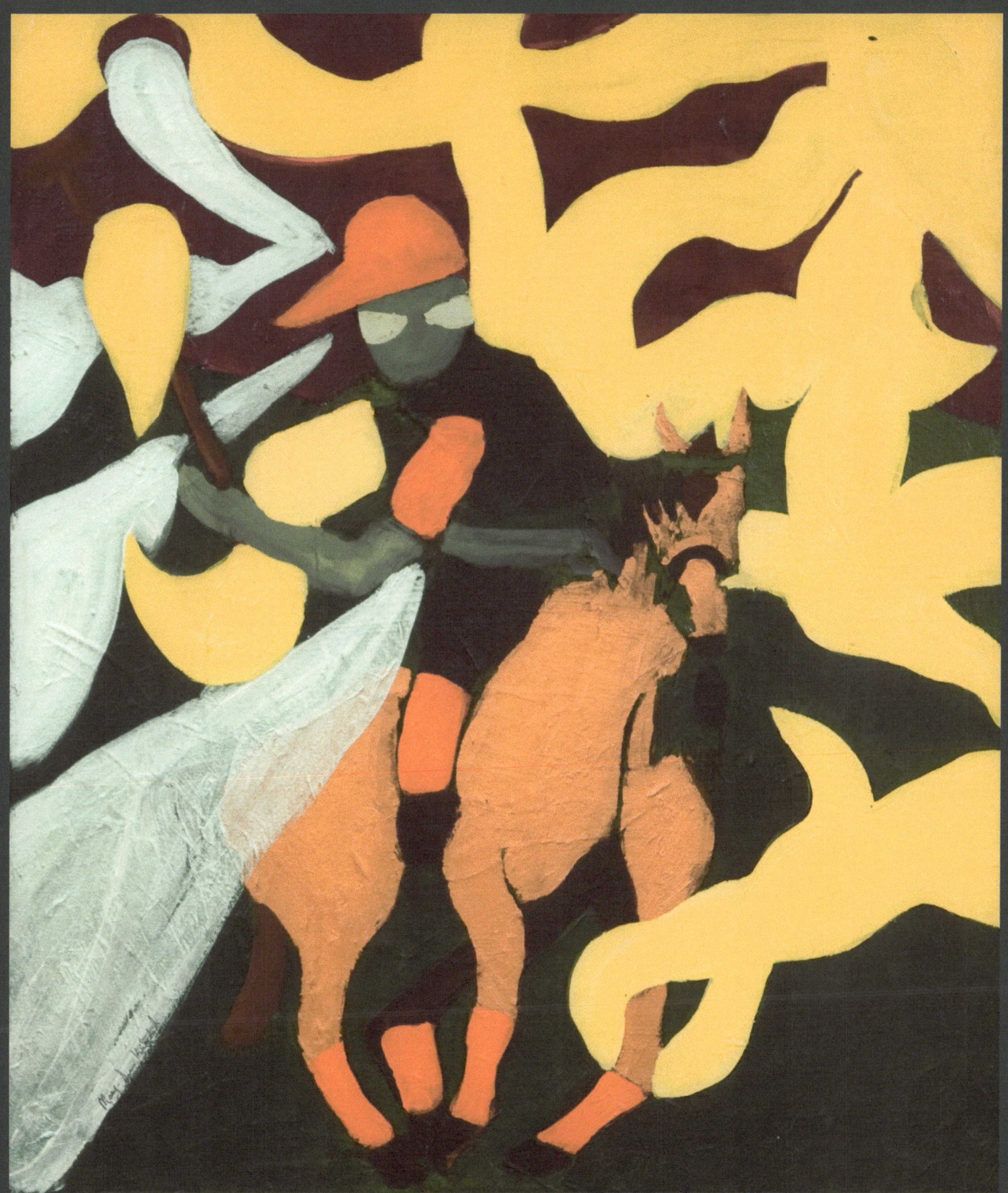

THE DAISIES AROUND MY WRIST
PERENNIAL THEY WILL ALWAYS BE
LIKE THE ONES WHO CANNOT TOUCH
BUT ONLY SEE

SEEDS OF MORNING GLORY
1993
ACRYLIC ON CANVAS
48 X 48 IN

SENIOR STUDIO THESIS EXHIBITION
HUNT-CAVANAGH GALLERY
SPRING 1993

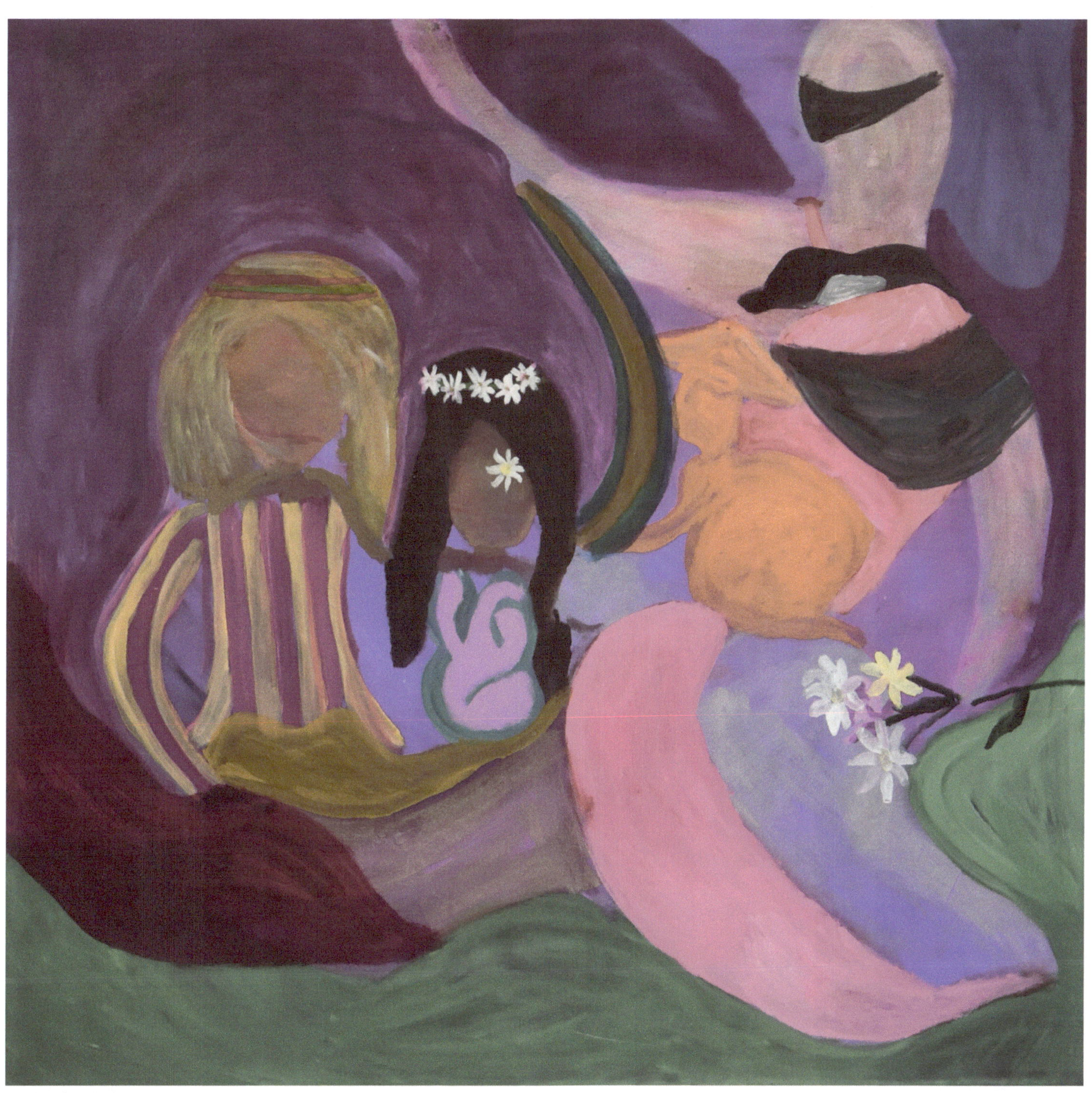

In the mirror
I see my reflection
In my eyes
I see my connection
In the mirror
I see my twin
In my eyes
I see me within

My Reflection
2001
Acrylic on canvas
36 x 13 in

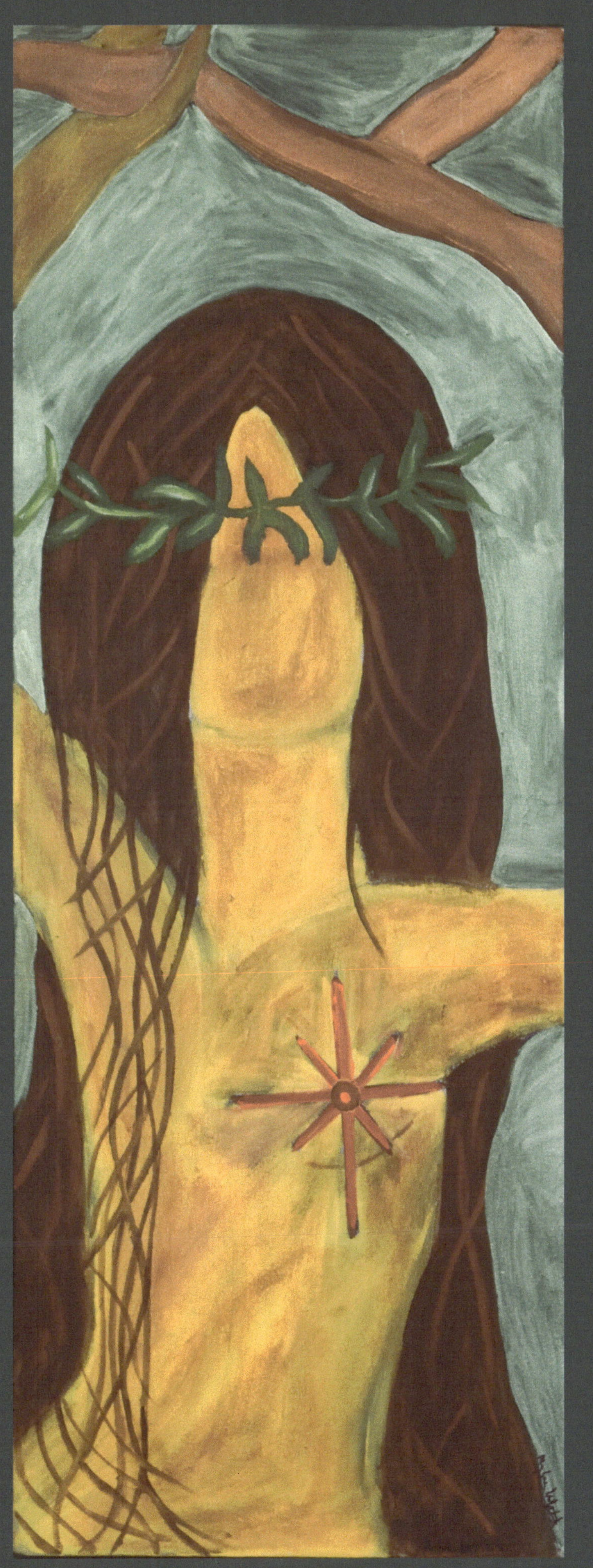

STRENGTH FORMING
THROUGHOUT THE INNER MARROW OF MY BONE
RED BLOOD CELLS REJUVENATING
TO ONCE AGAIN BE GROWN
FEELING MYSELF BREATHE
AS IF IT WAS THE DAY OF MY BIRTH
JUST FROM DISCOVERING
THAT YOU EXIST ON THIS EARTH

REJUVENATION
2002
ACRYLIC ON CANVAS
60 X 48 IN

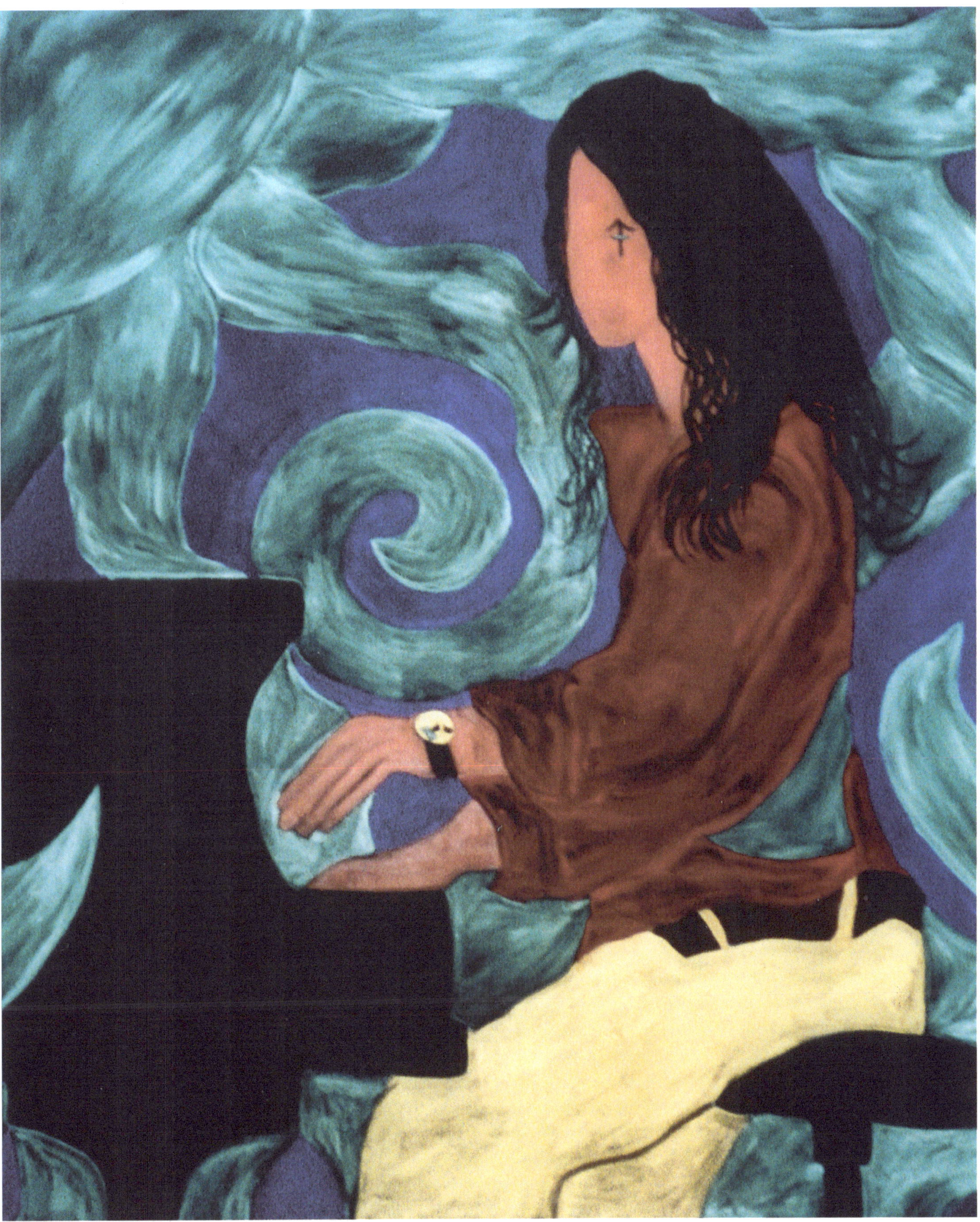

If you were a bat flyin' in the sky
I would throw all my garlic away
You would be the vampire
I would allow to stay

Stream
2008
Acrylic on canvas
15 x 30 in

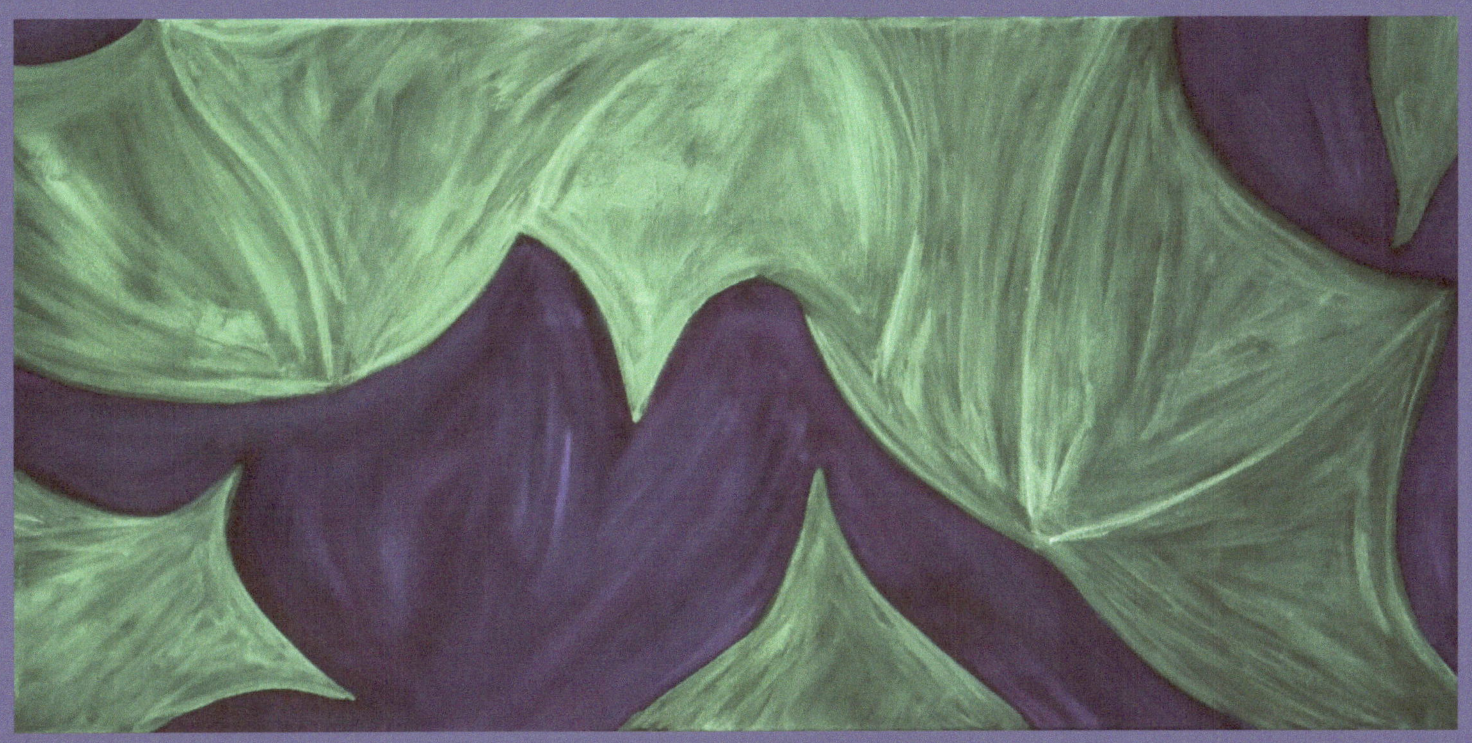

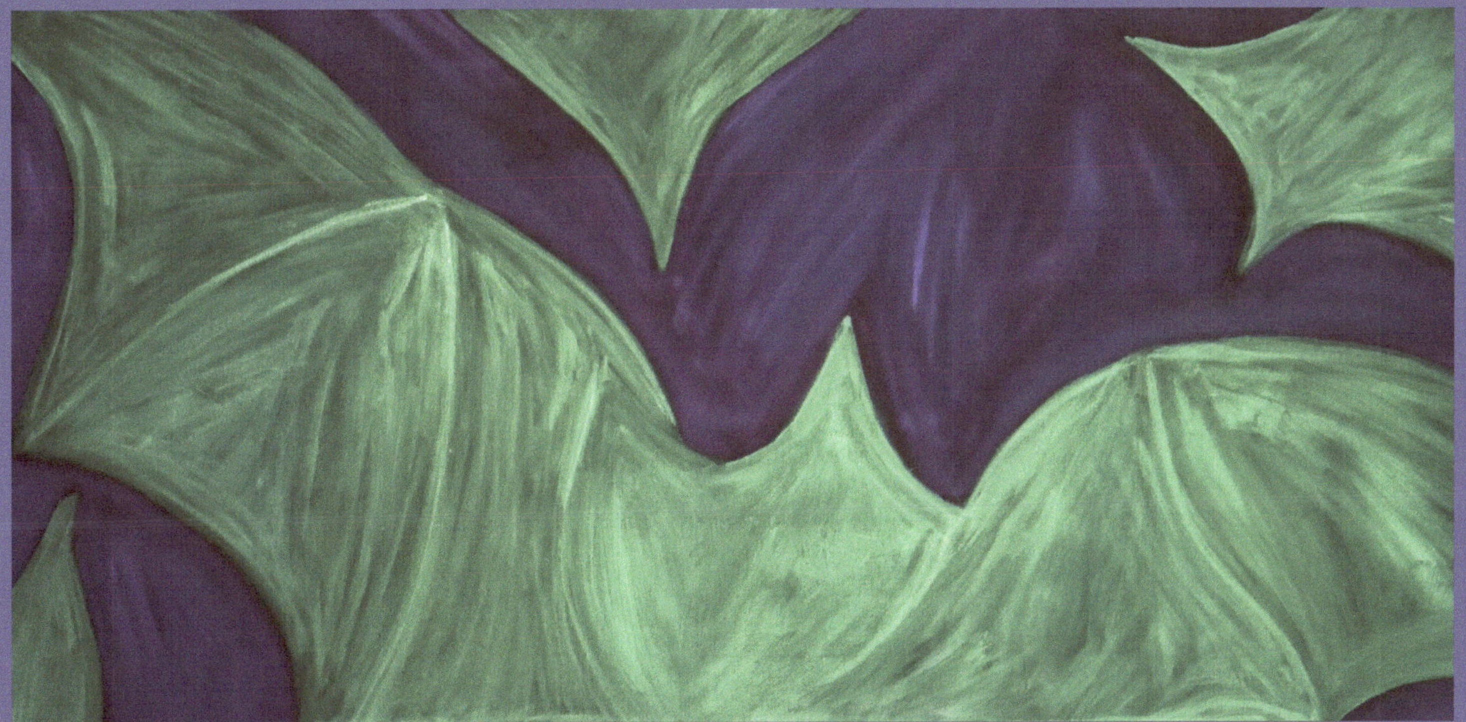

No longer are you here by flesh
sweet lizard king
guardian over all that sing
but you still speak your once in a lifetime mind
way ahead of the answers society is trying to find

December Daze
2001
Acrylic on canvas
50 x 46 in

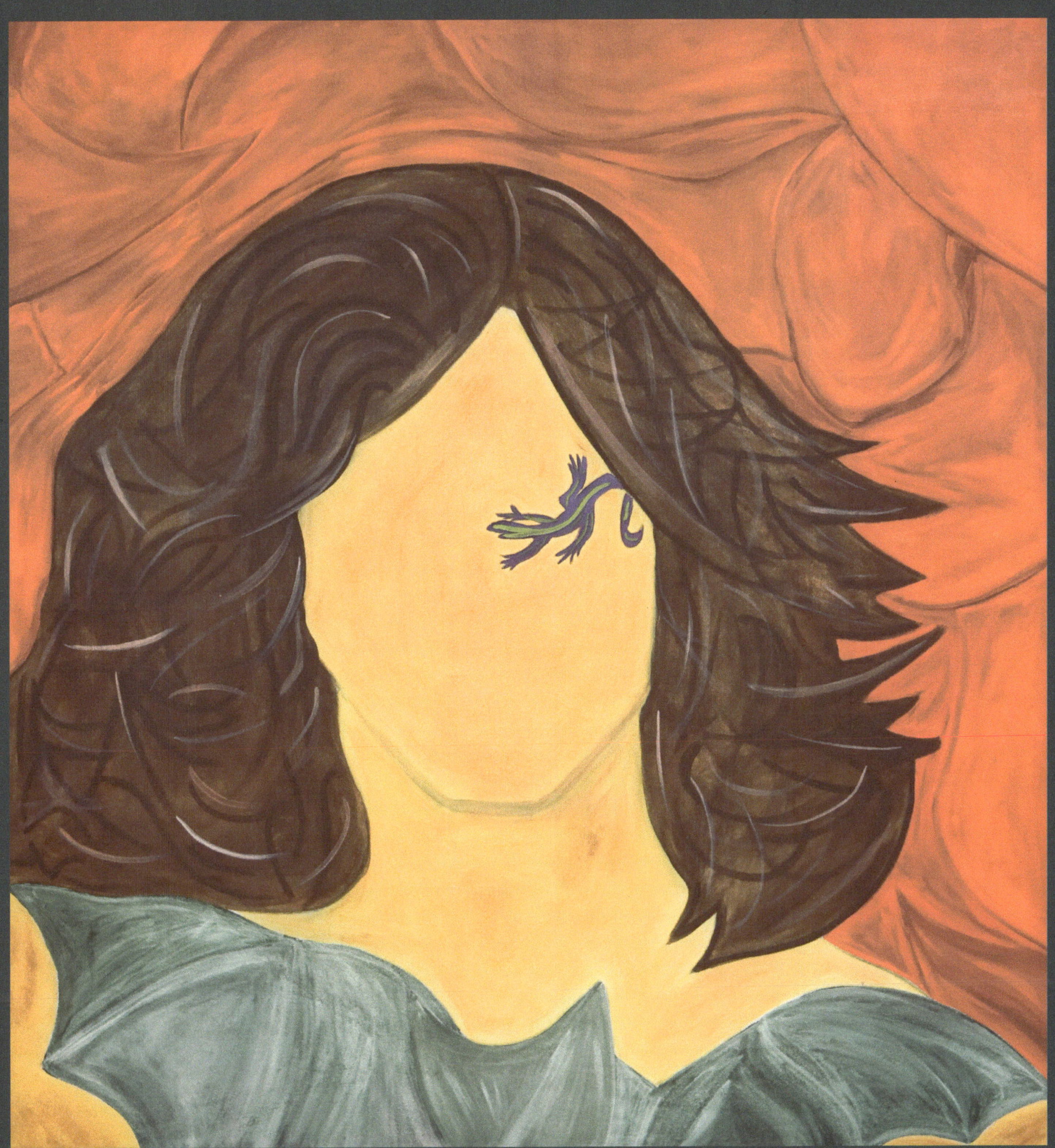

Clay

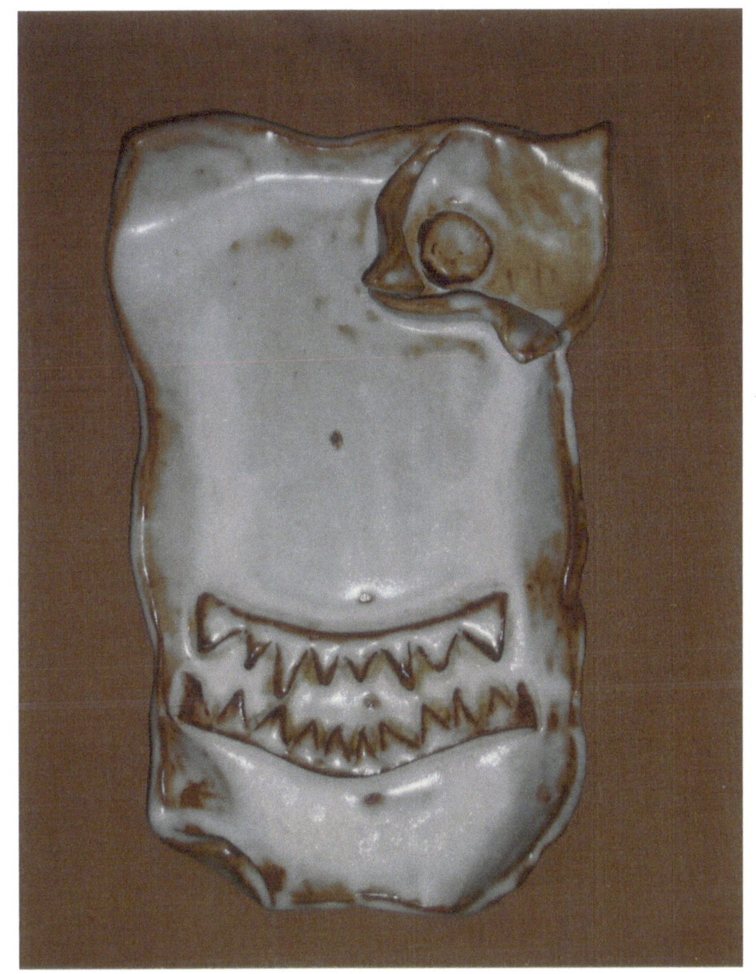

AUIMAITOK
1996
WATER FOUNTAIN
MAT GLAZE

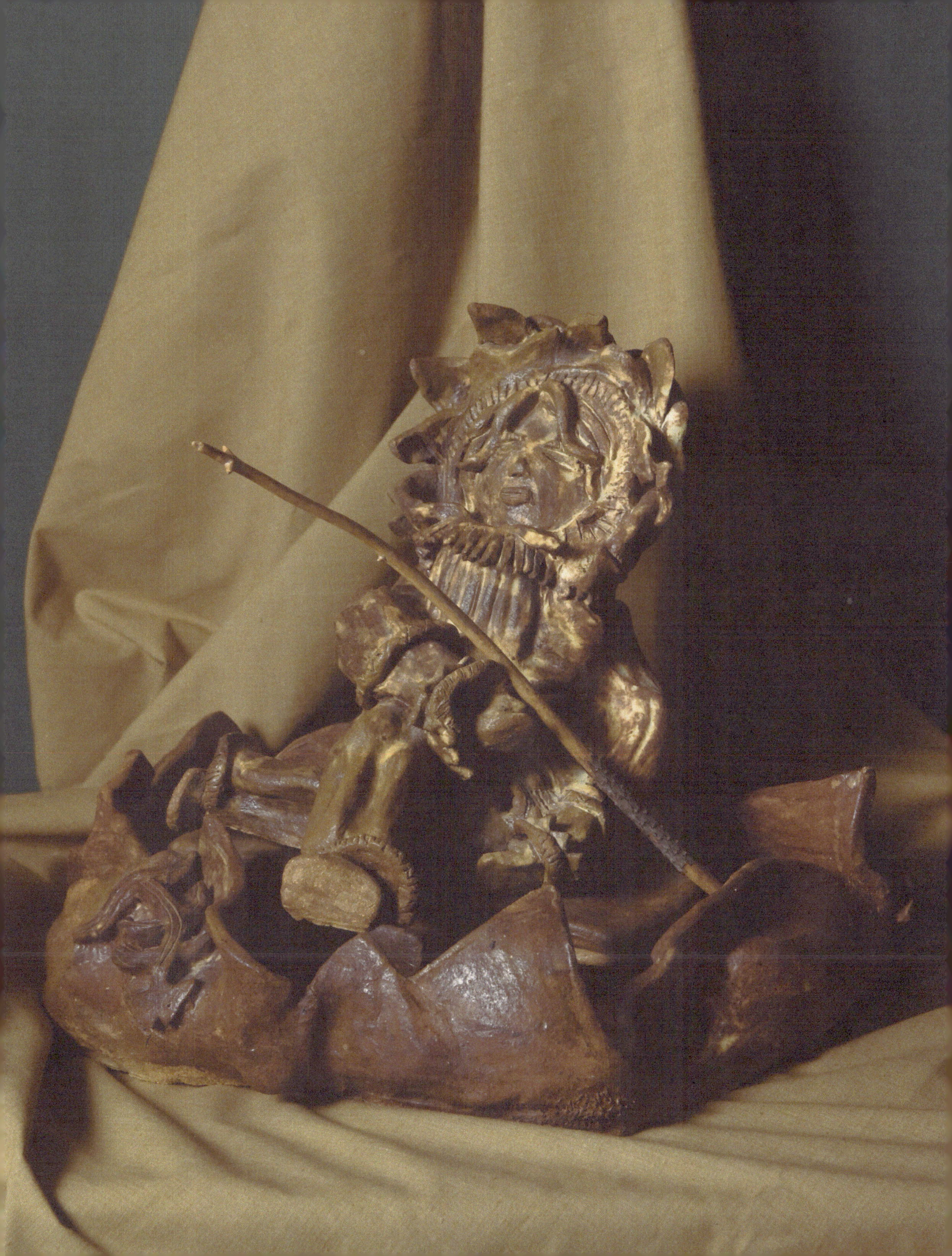

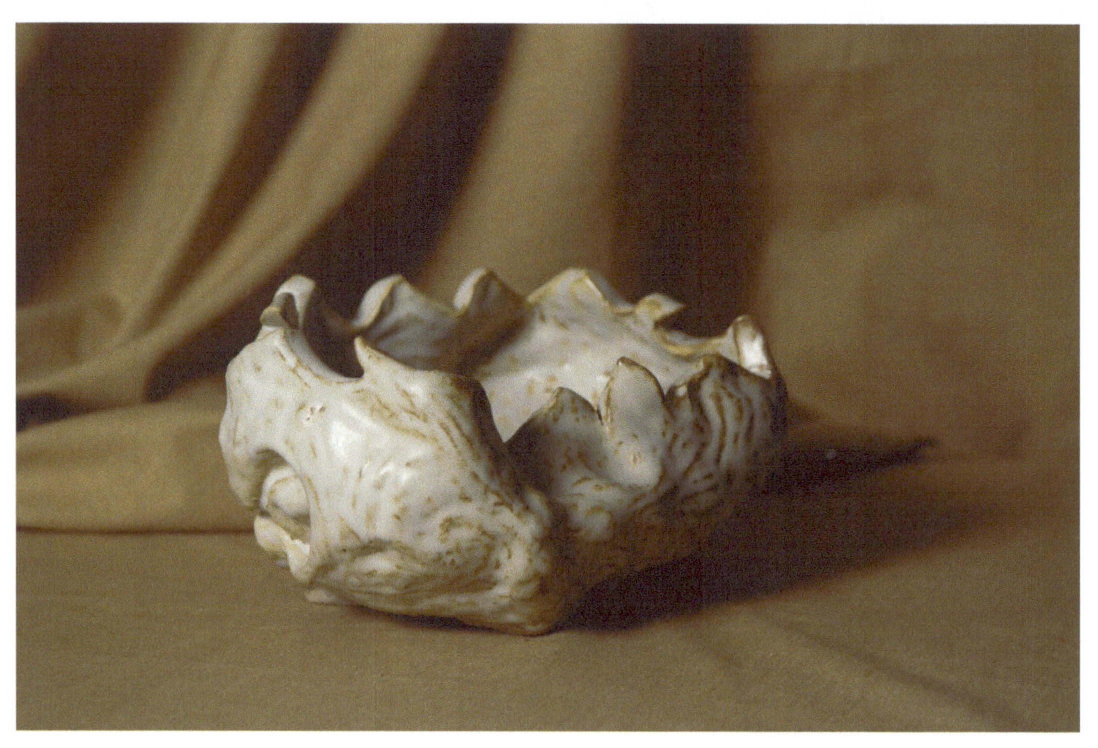

ARIZONA SHOCK
1995
BOWL
MAT GLAZE

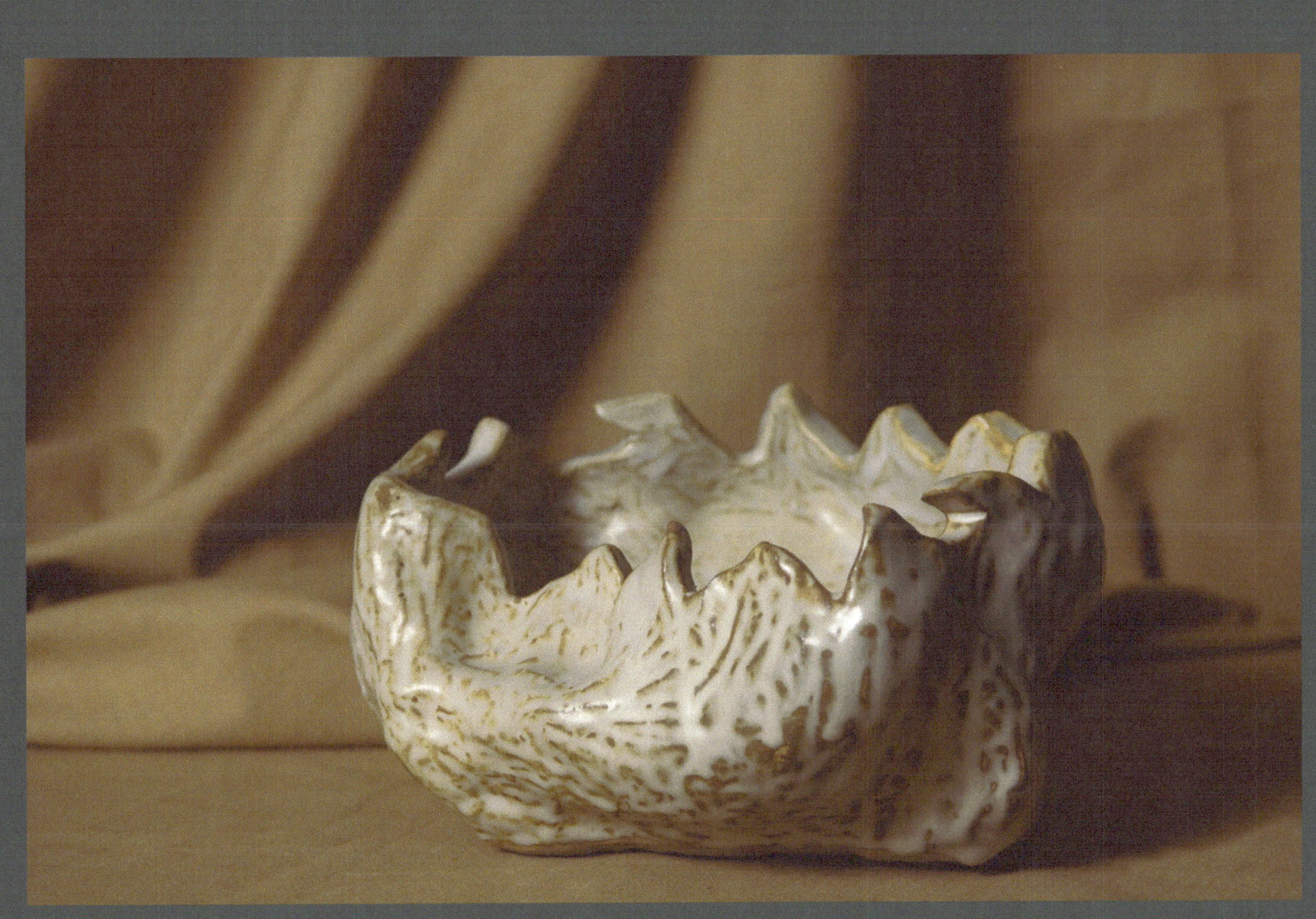

EMBRACE THE TRADE WINDS
1995
VASE
MAT GLAZE

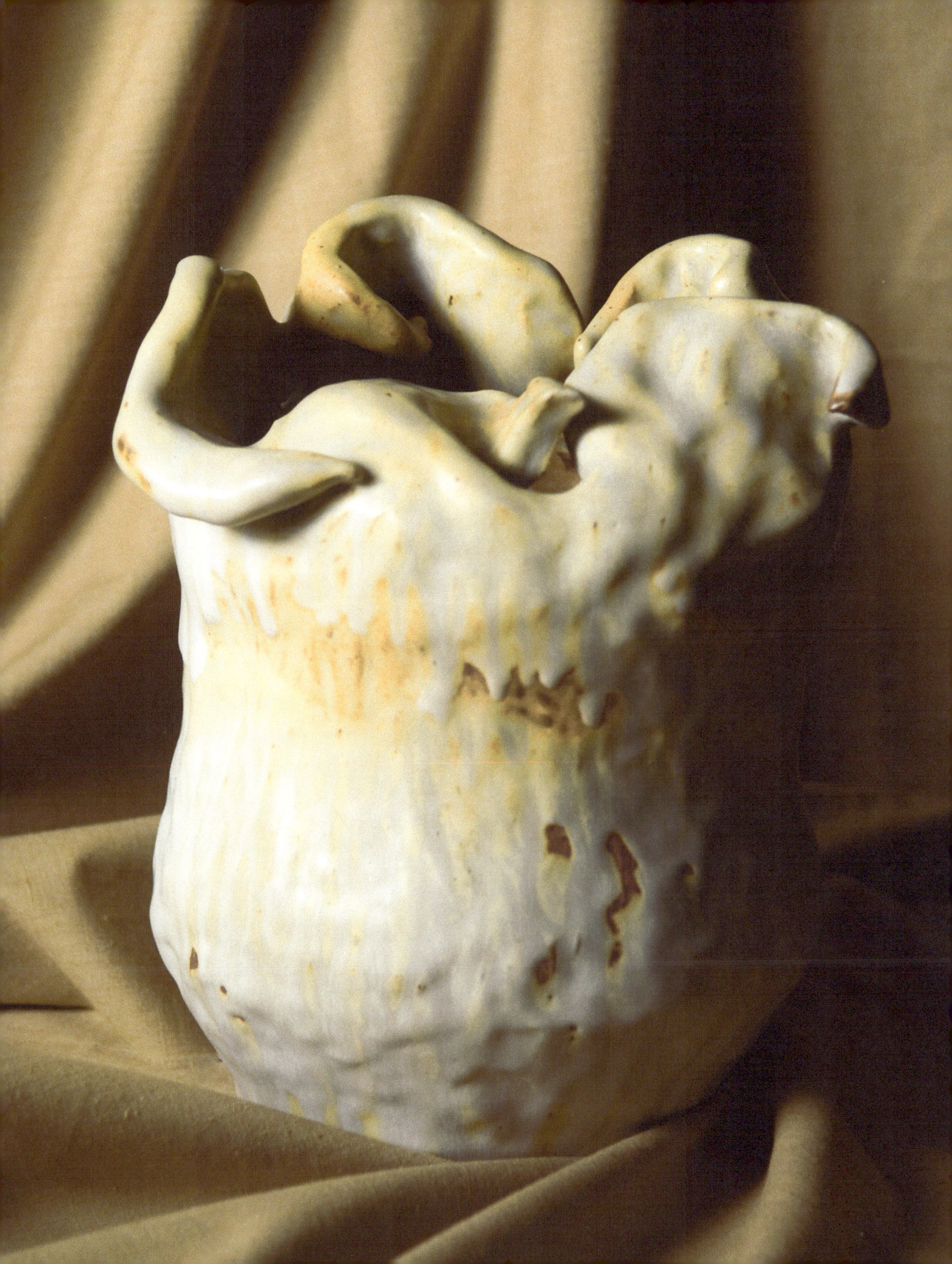

CHARLESTON TIDE
1995
VASE
MAT GLAZE

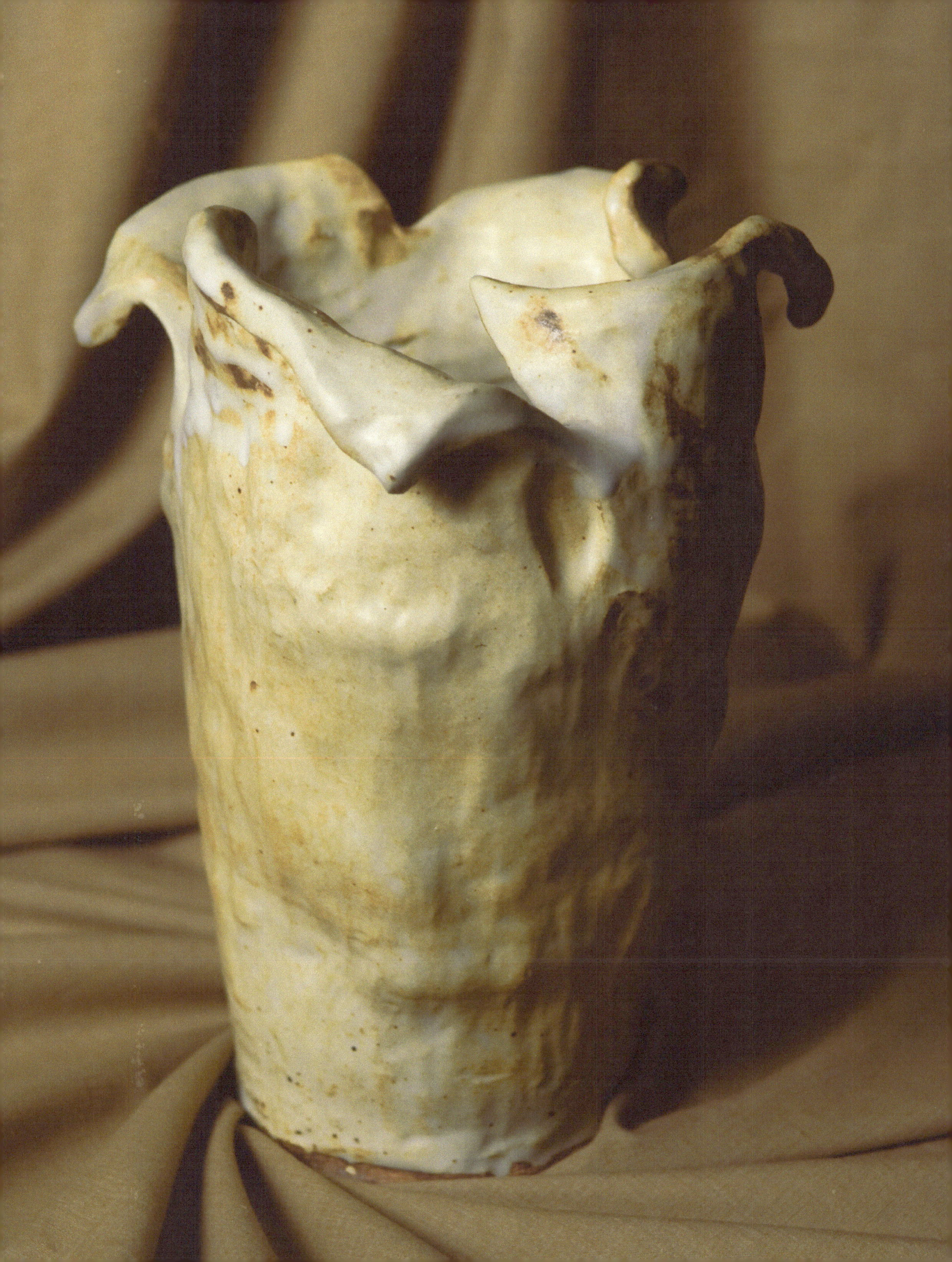

OUTERBANK CLIFF
1995
VASE
MAT GLAZE

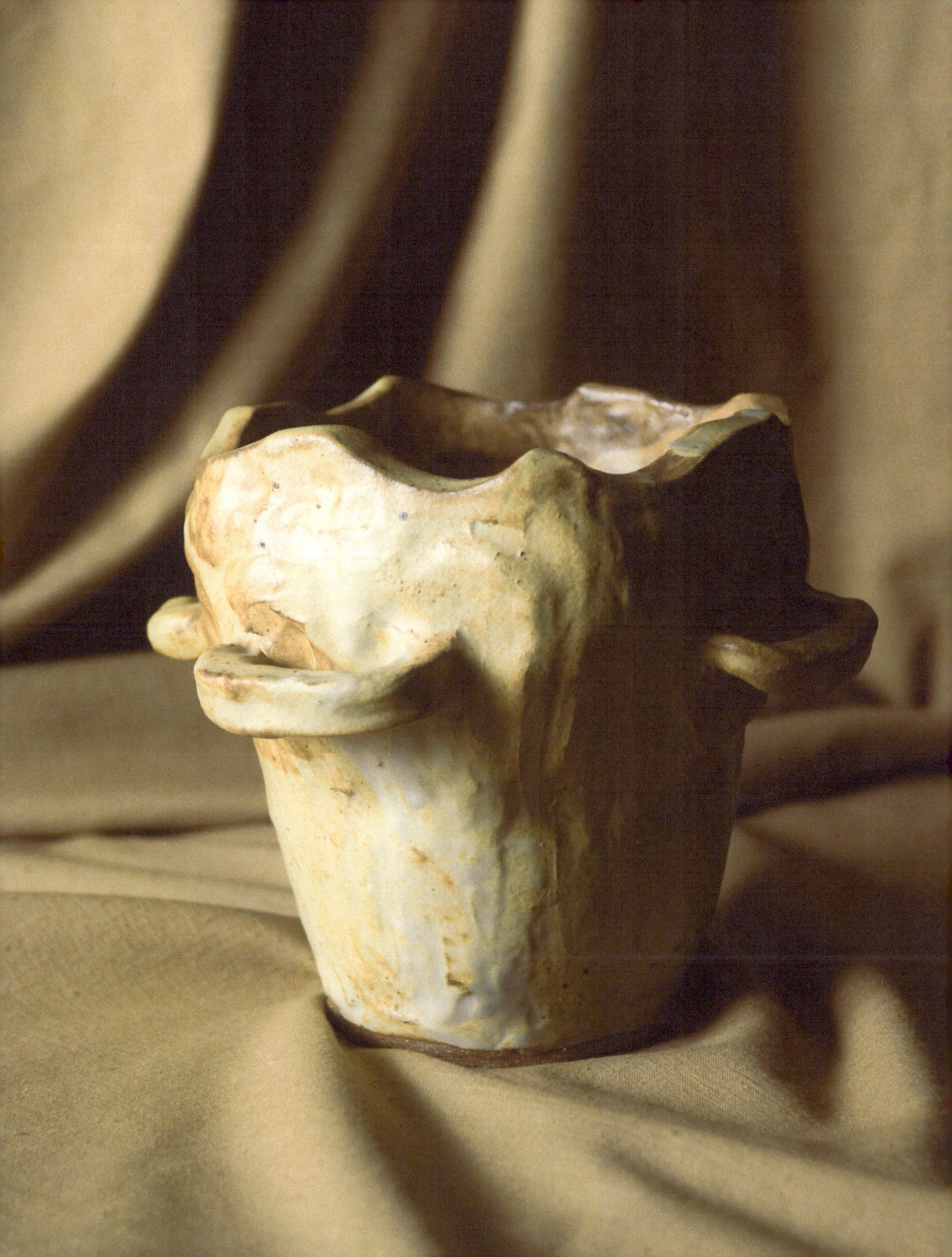

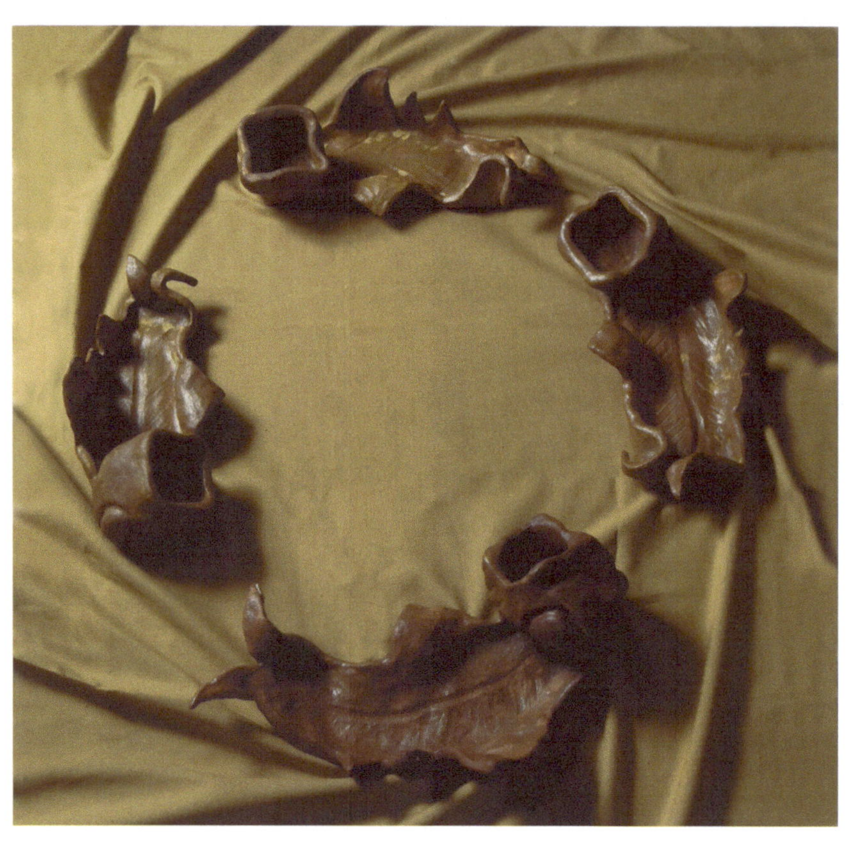

RIVER SPLASH TUESDAY
1996
SET OF FOUR PLATES
MAT GLAZE

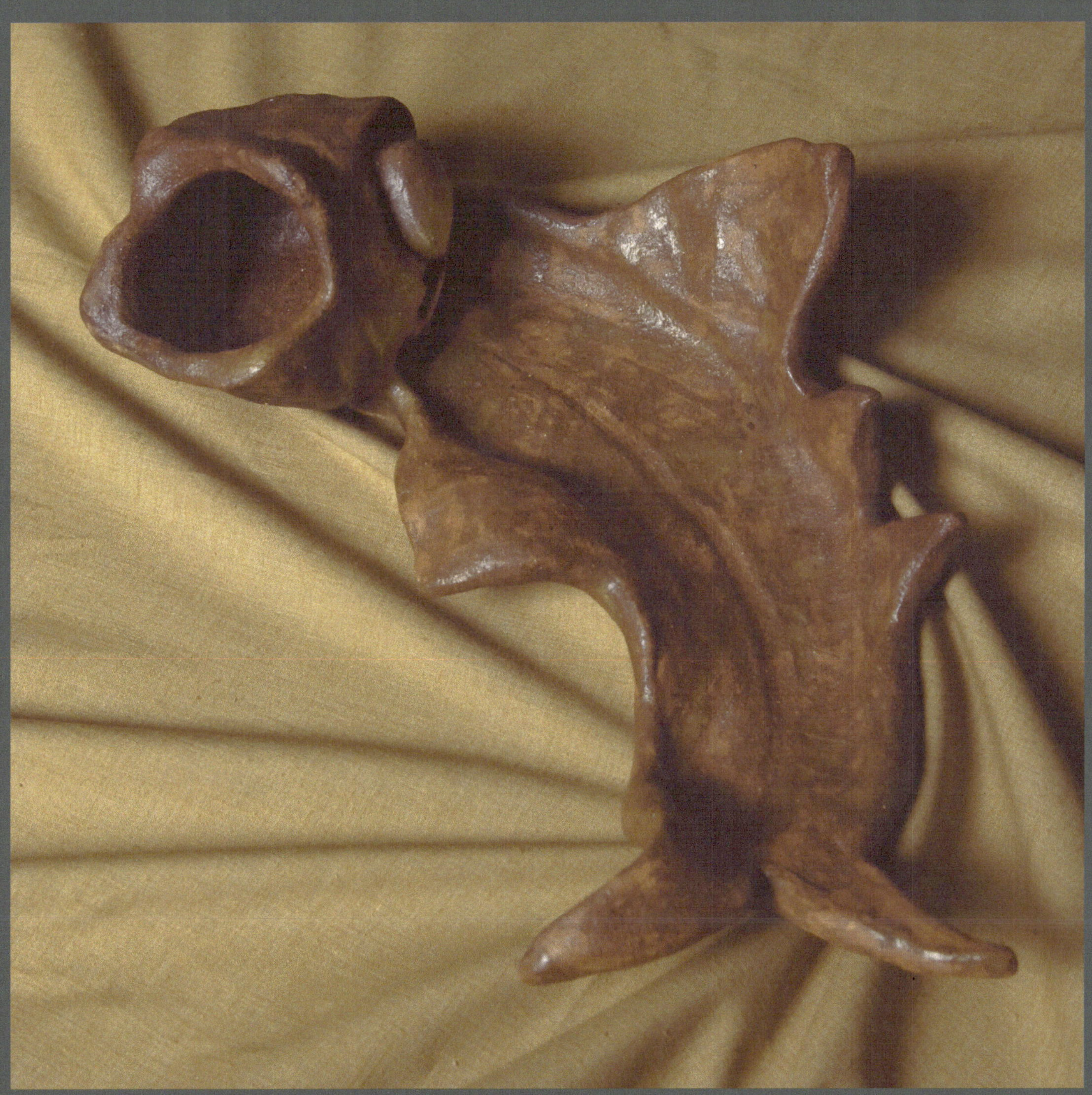

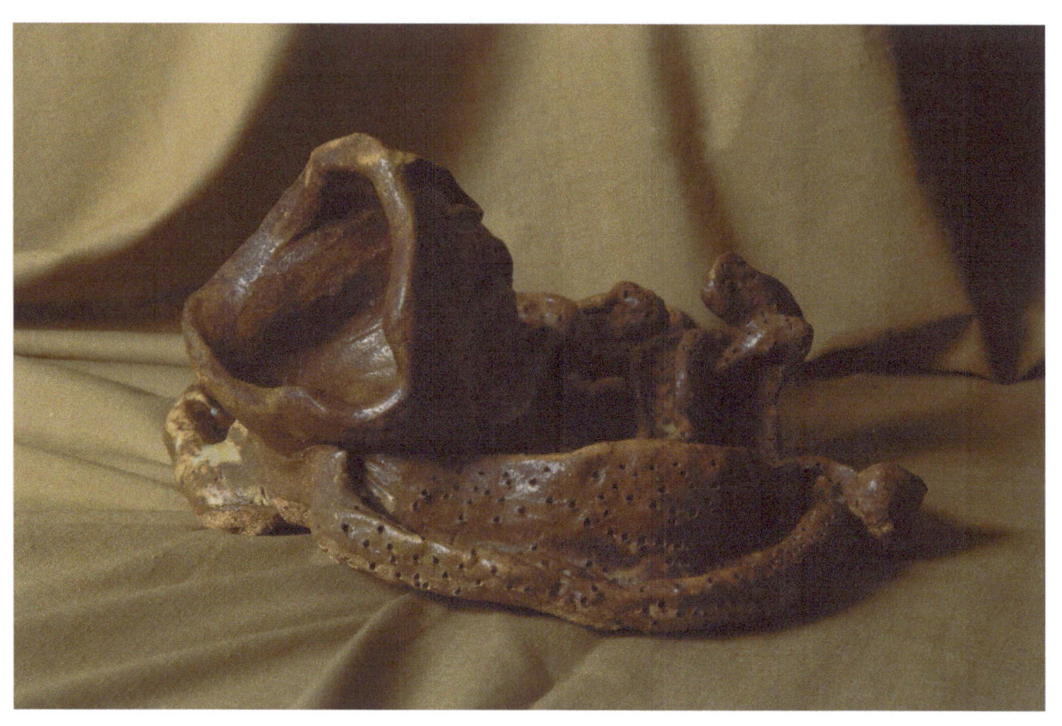

BENEATH KAHUKU
1996
SCULPTURE AND HORS D'OEUVRES
MAT GLAZE

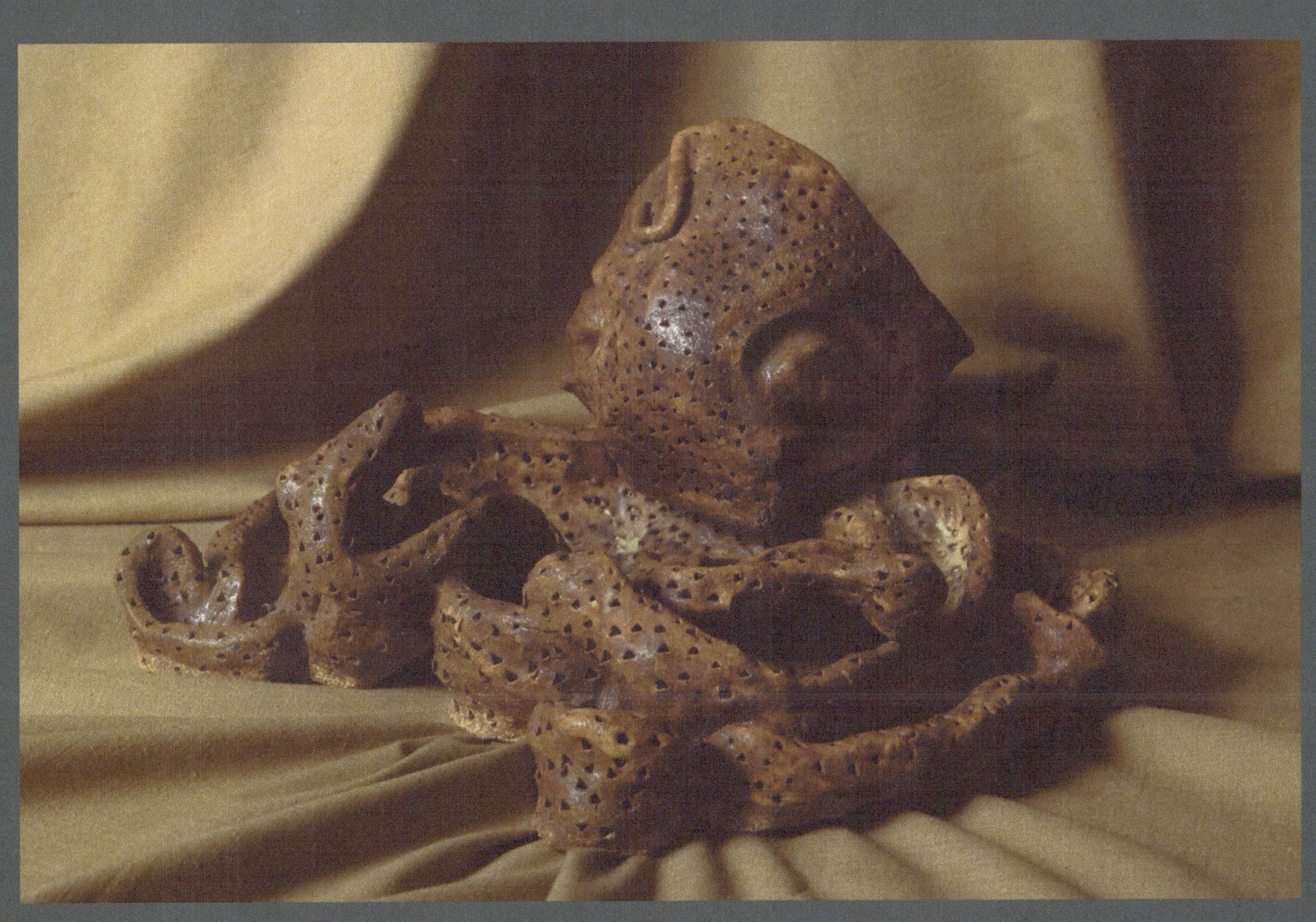

KAUAI ABYSS
1995
DIVIDED BOWL
MAT GLAZE

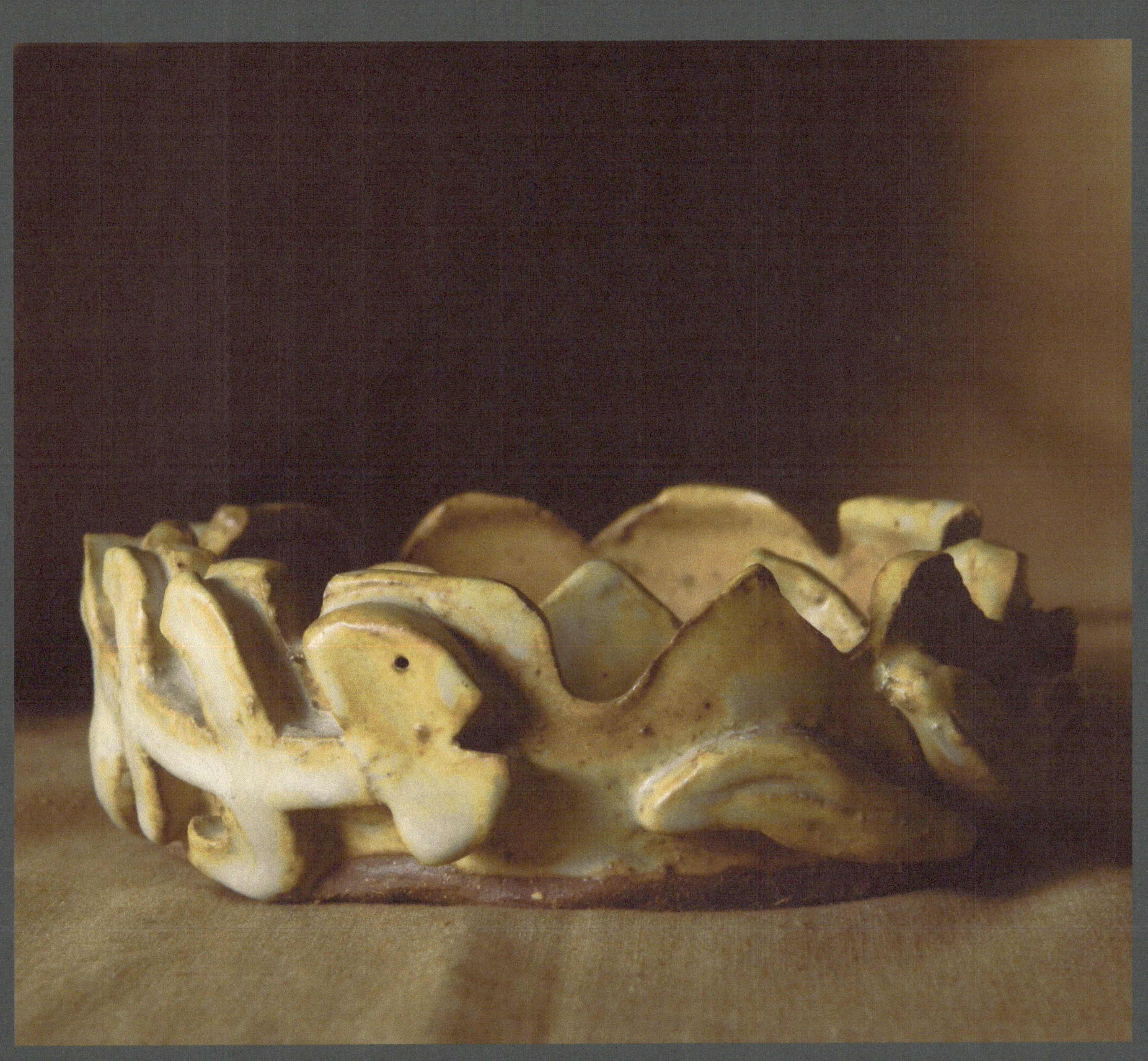

HALEIWA HIDEAWAY
1995
BOWL
MAT GLAZE

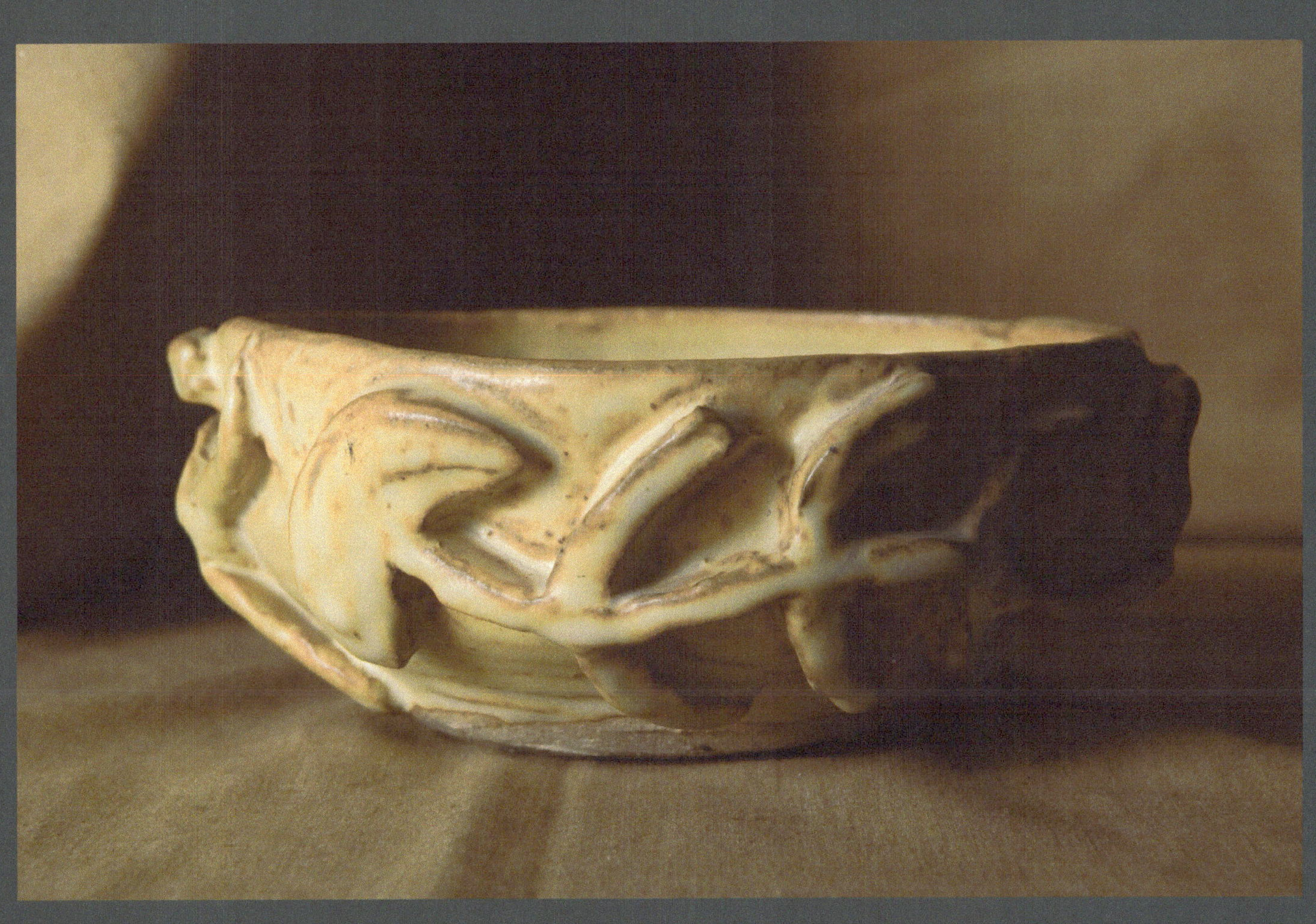

HANALEI SWIRL
1995
BOWL
MAT GLAZE

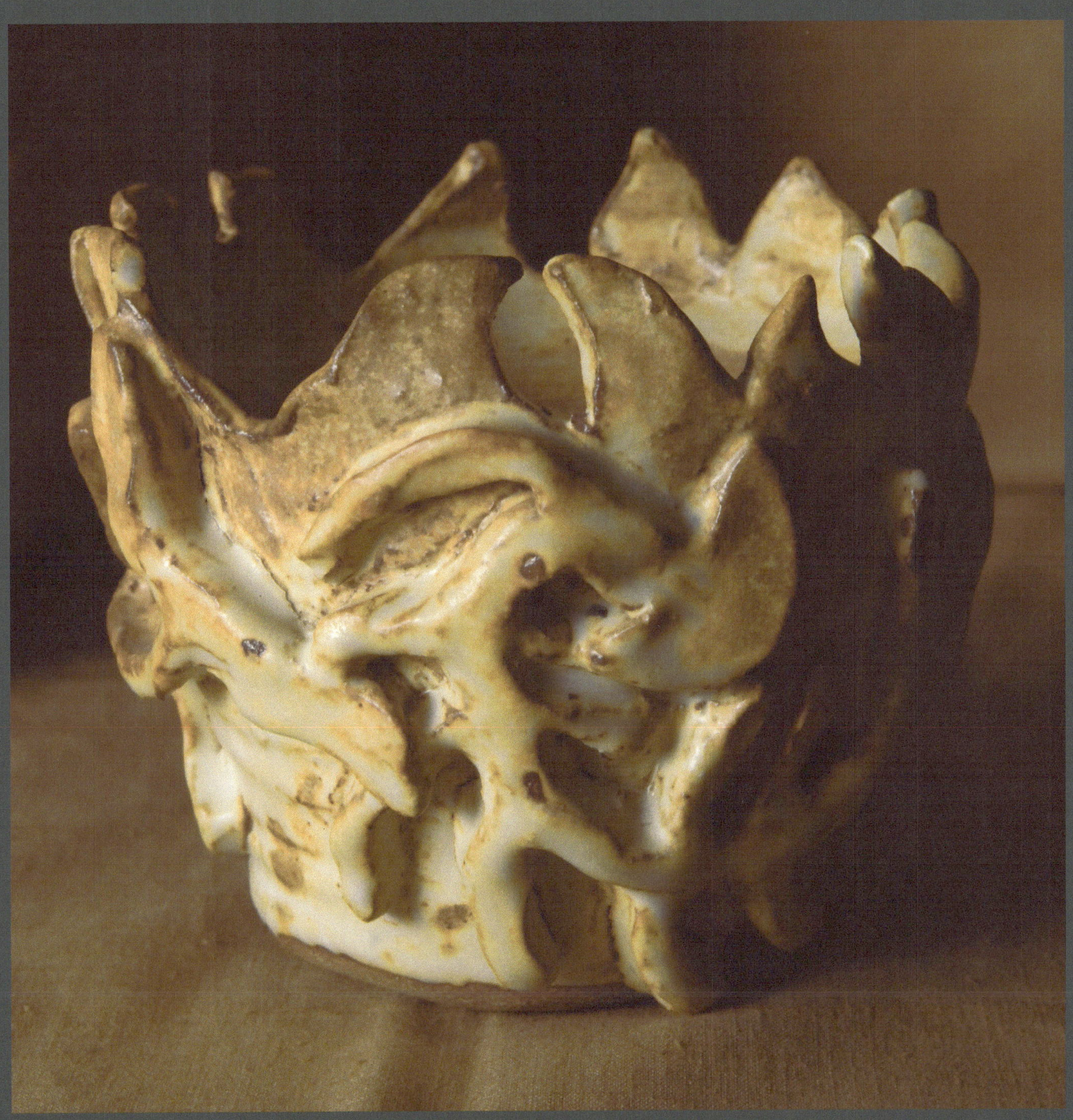

RUGGED RANGE
1995
MAT GLAZE

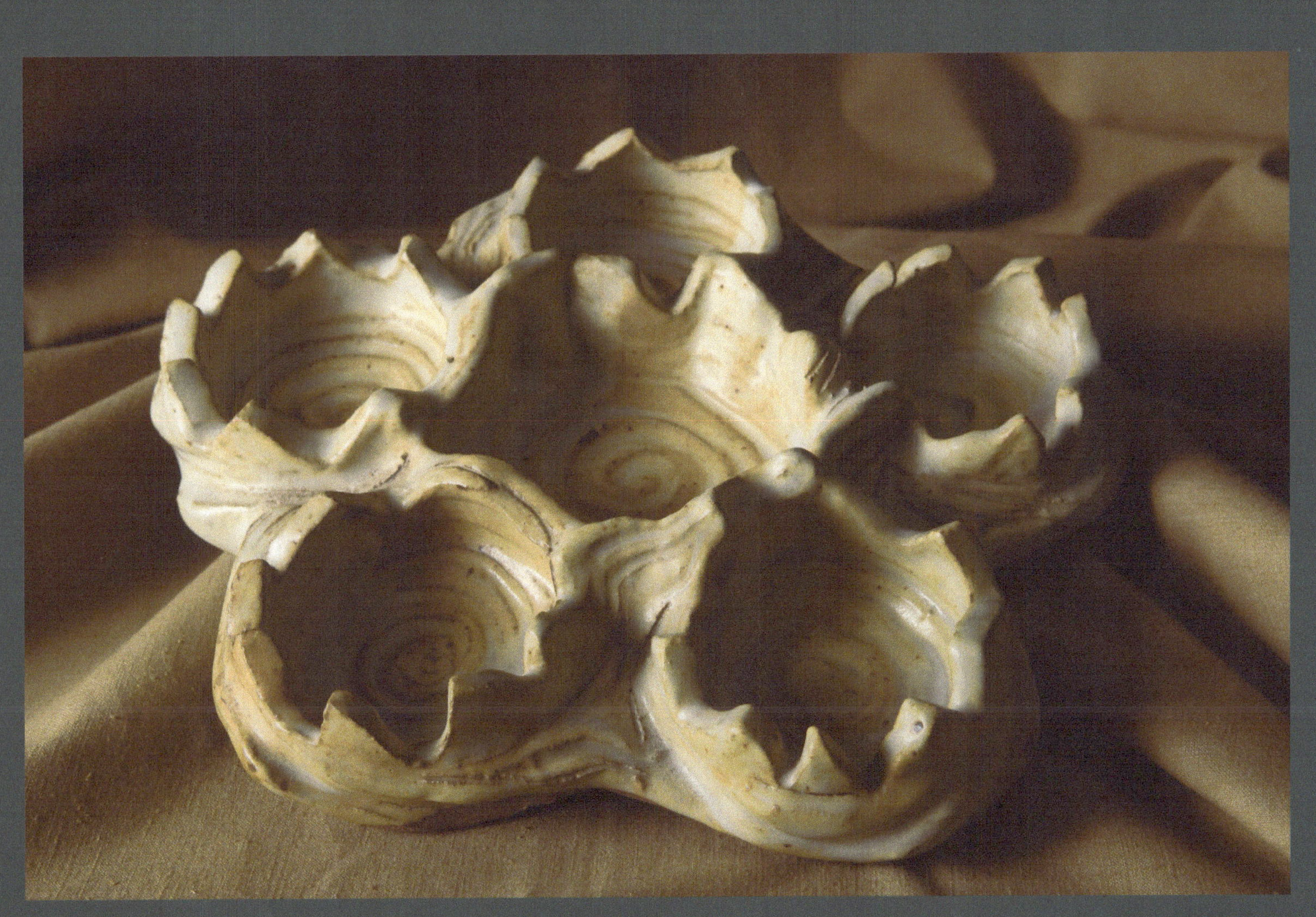

TURTLE FLIP
1995
BOWL
MAT GLAZE

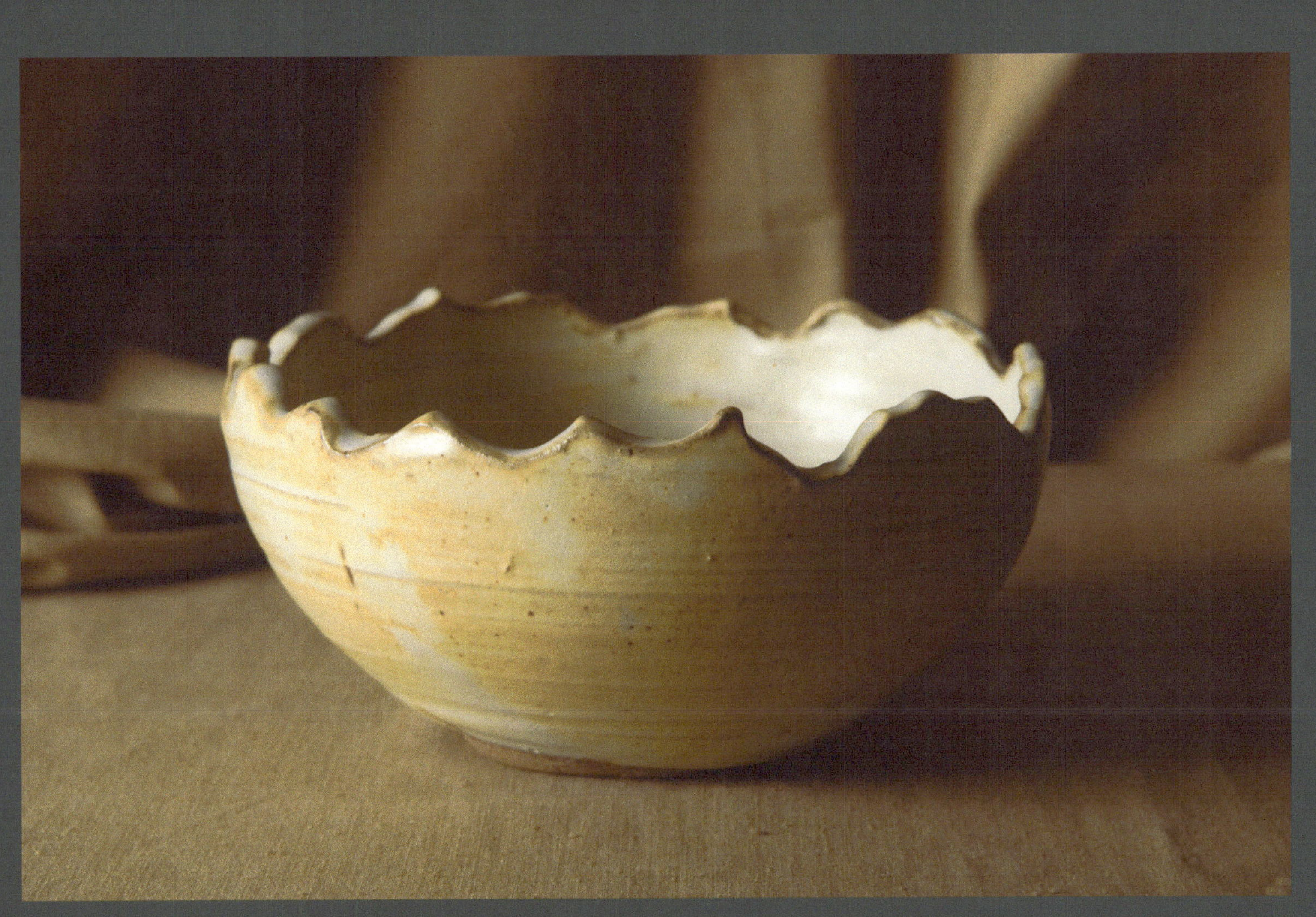

HI THERE SUGAR!
1995
TWO PIECE SET
MAT GLAZE

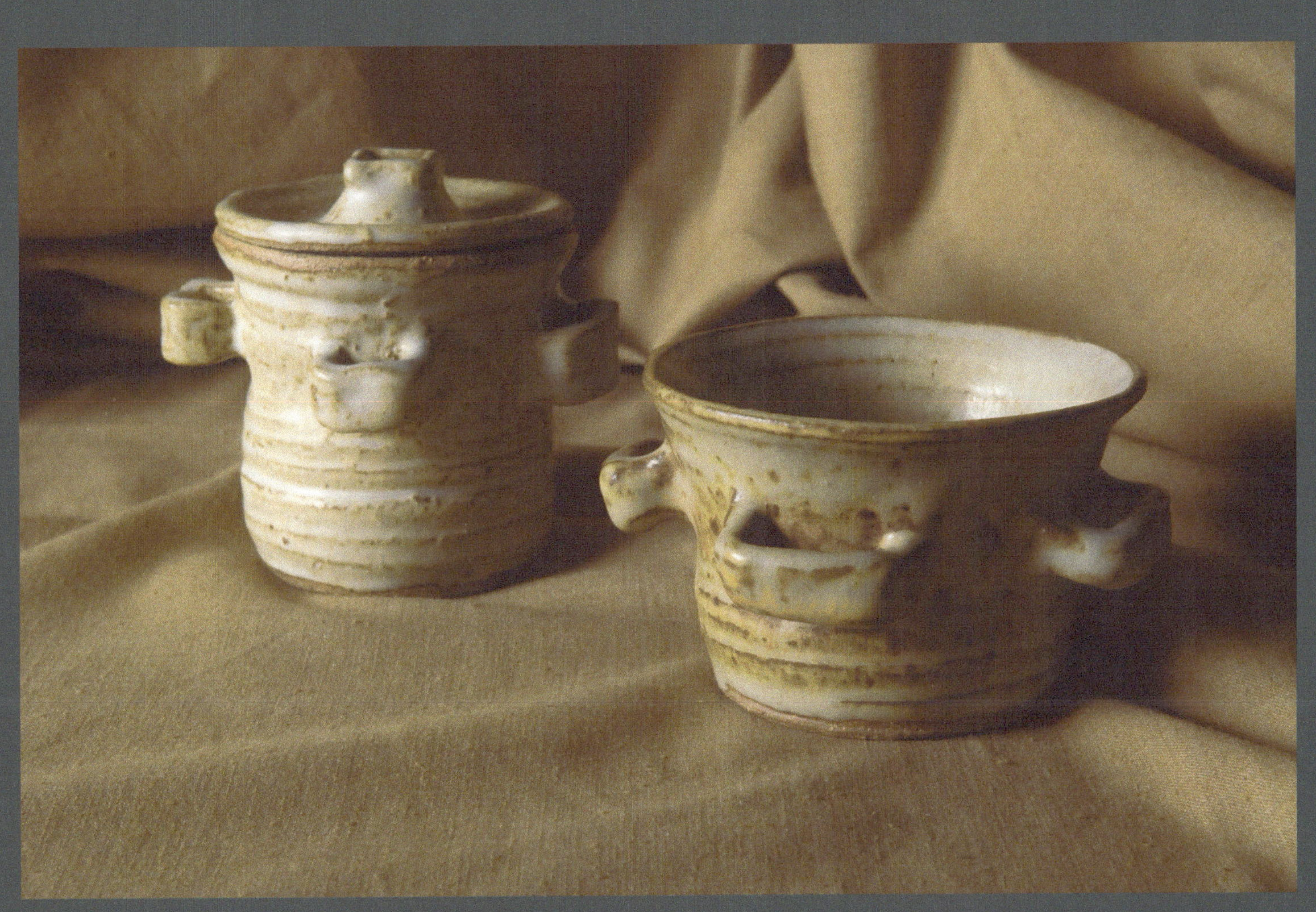

RIDGE OF THE BUTTERFLY
1995
TIPI MOBILE
MAT GLAZE

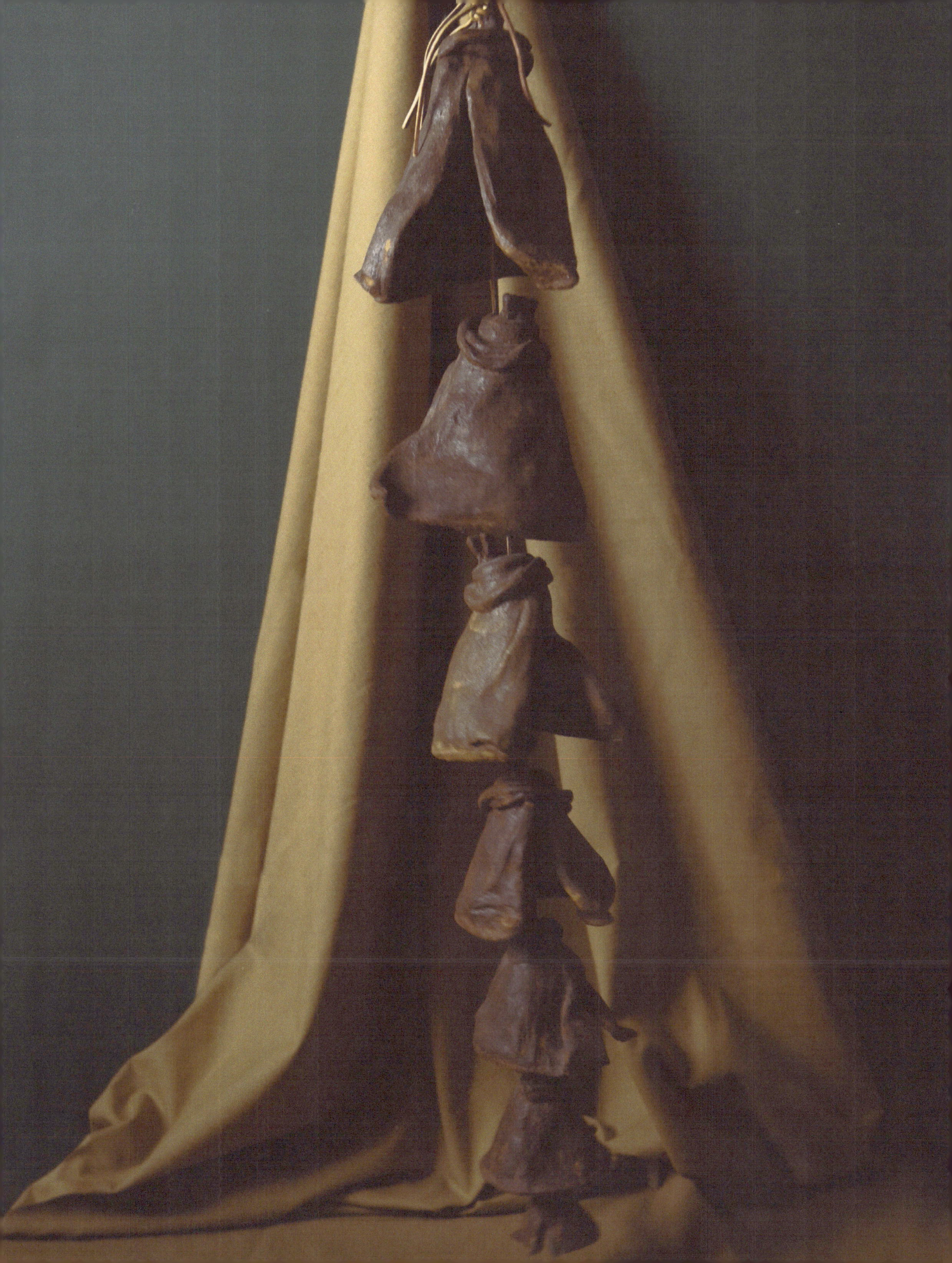

BROOK
1995
MAT GLAZE

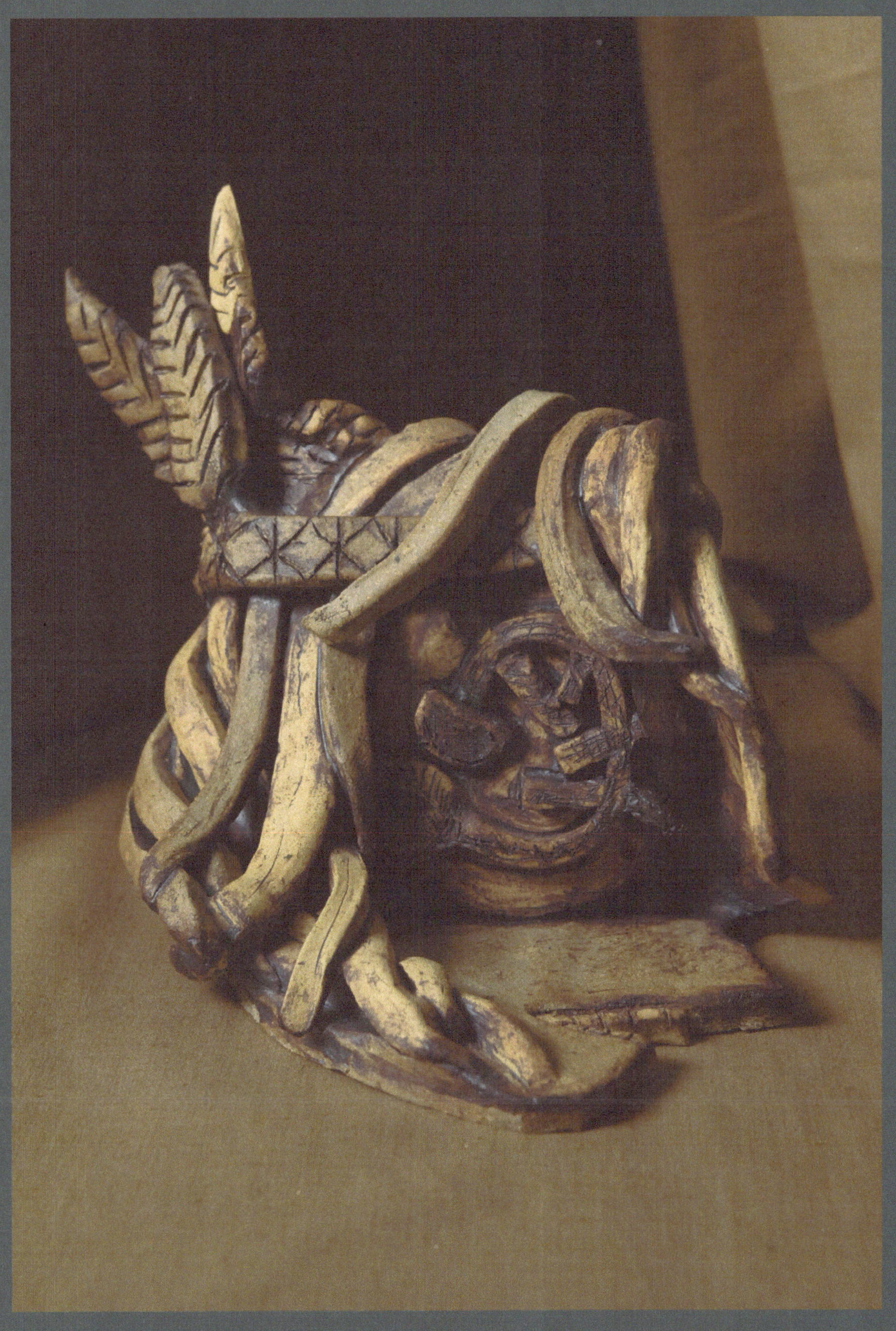

MAGNOLIA FLAT
1995
SET OF TWO
MAT GLAZE

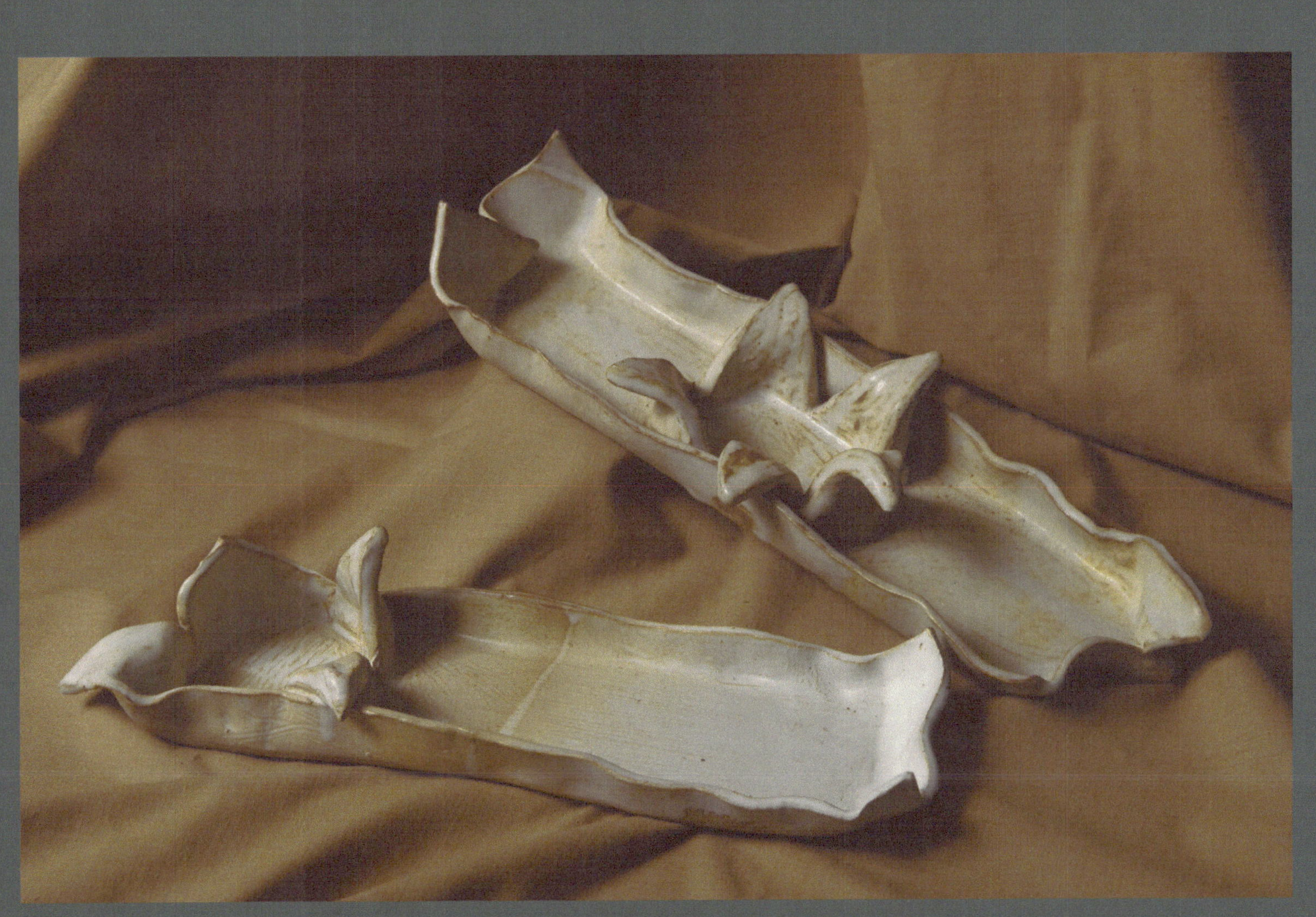

SASSAFRAS HUG
1995
MAT GLAZE

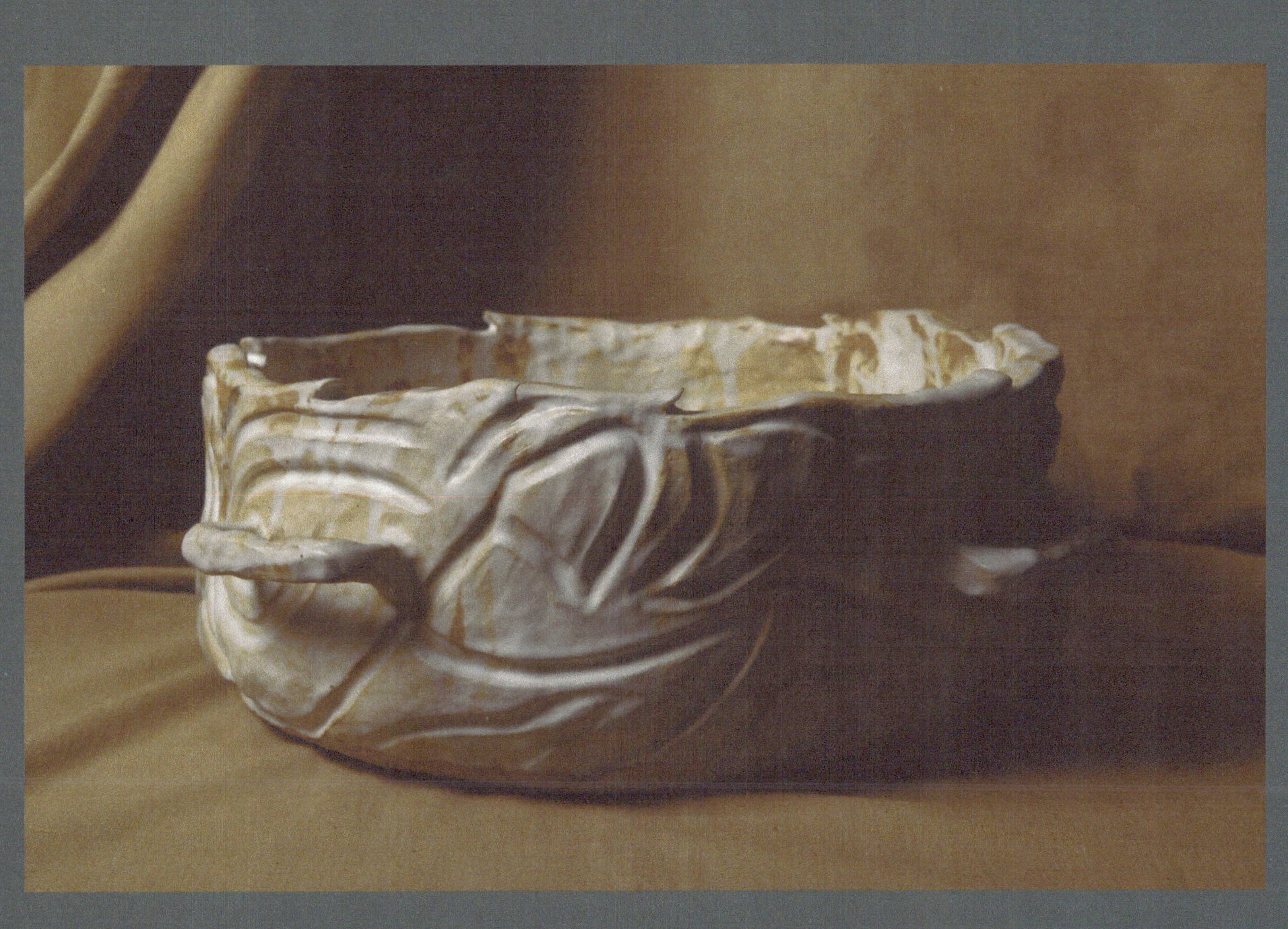

SUMTER SPRING
1995
SERVING DISH
MAT GLAZE

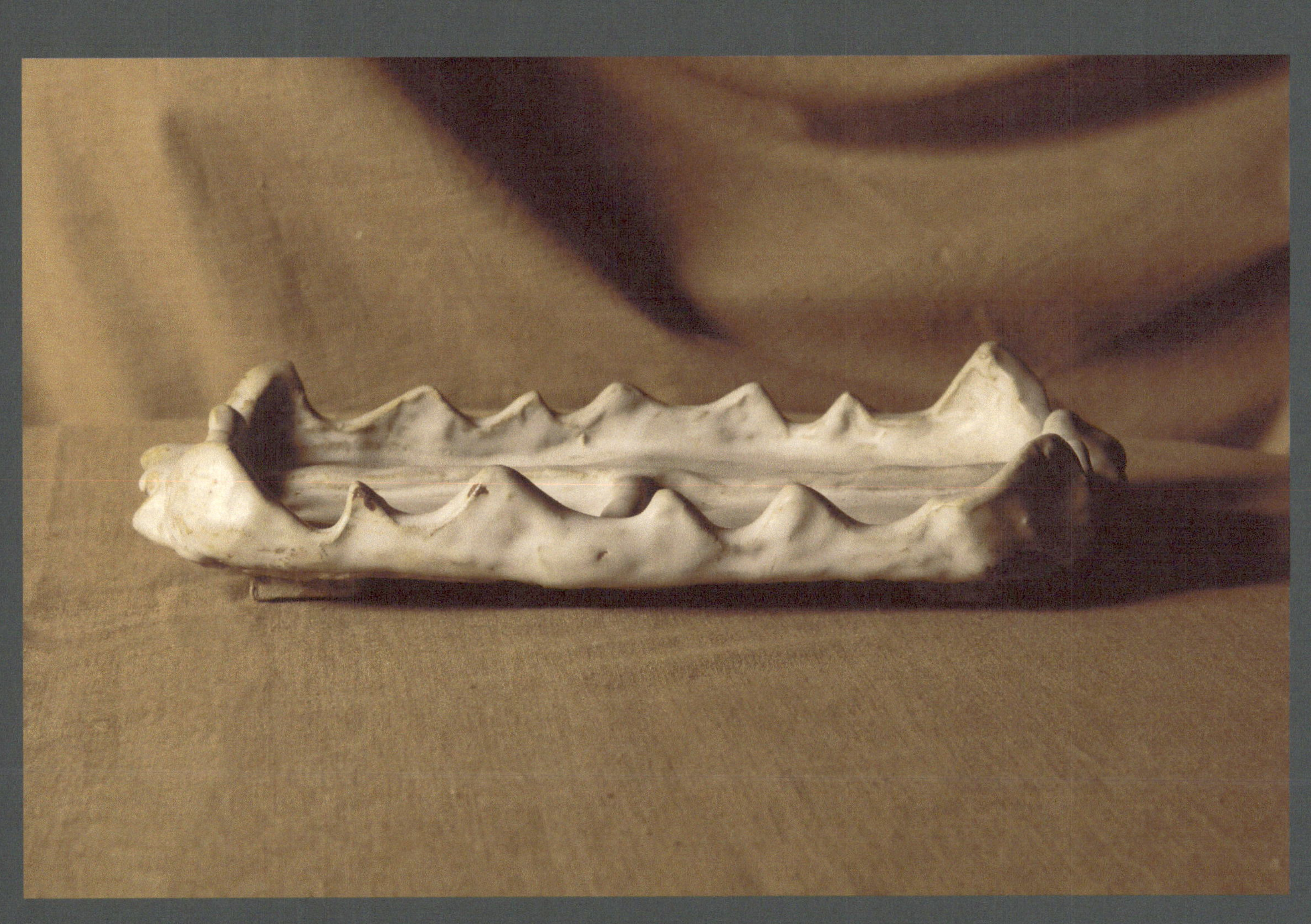

CARTERSVILLE CREEK
1995
SERVING DISH
MAT GLAZE

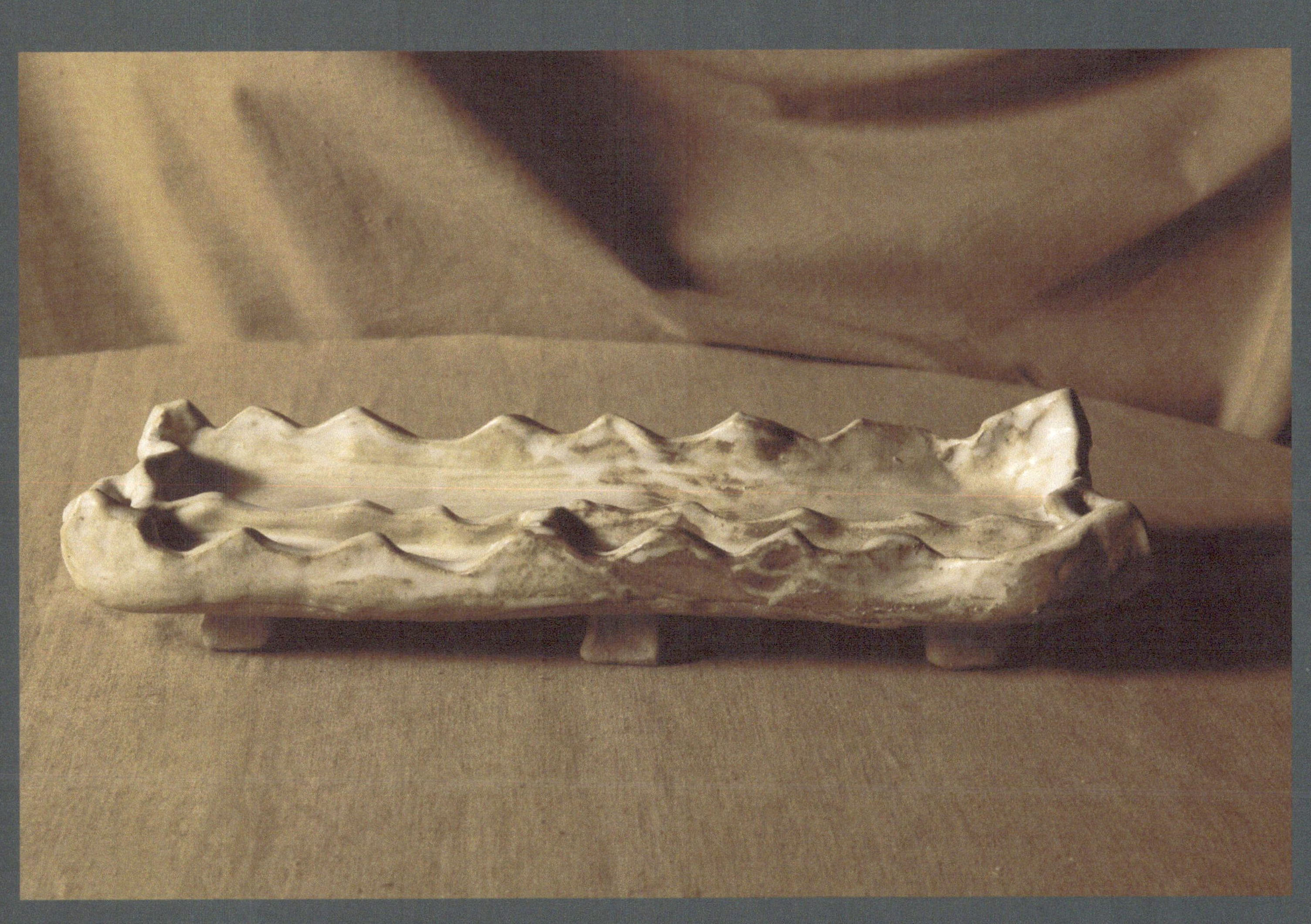

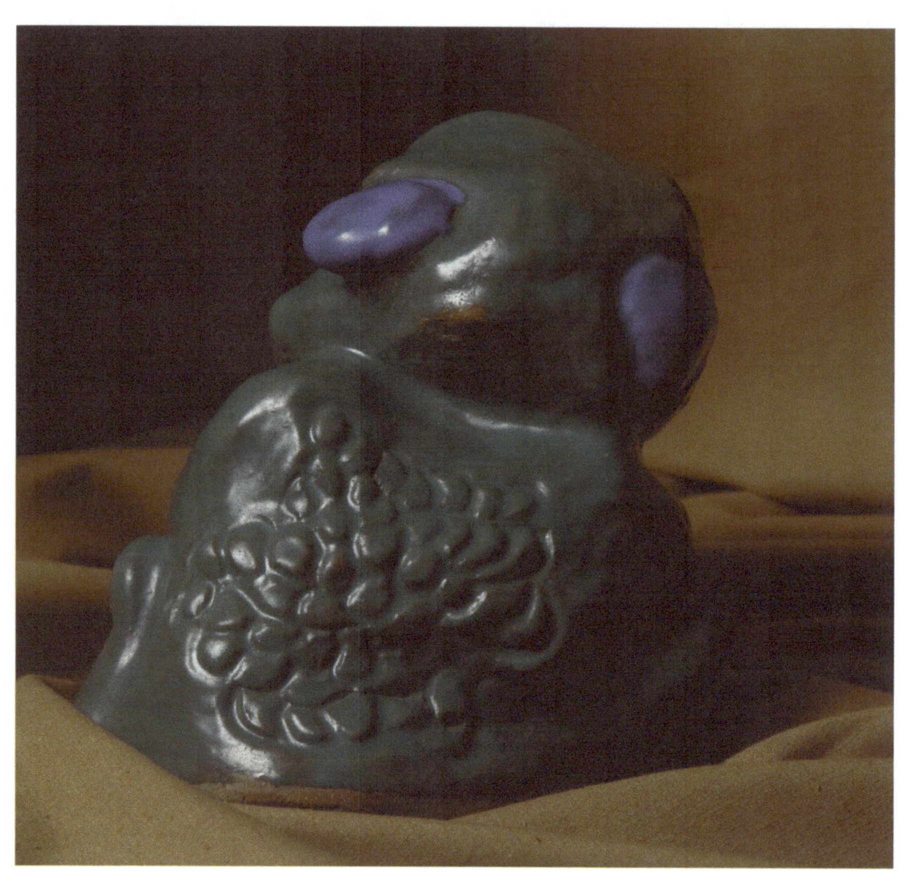

BIRMINGHAM
1996
CITRUS HOLDER
MAT GLAZE

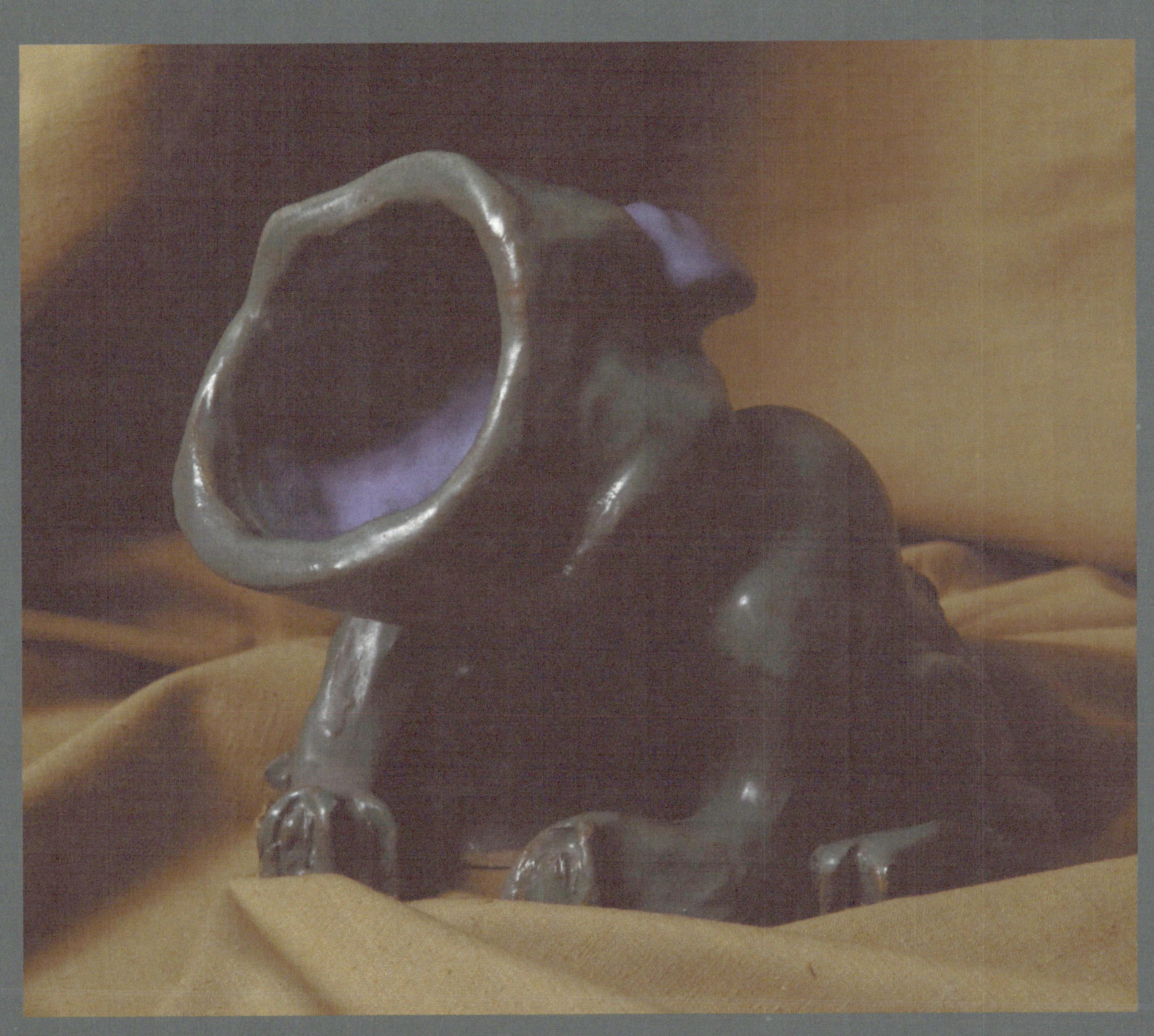

PAINT

CLAY

POETRY

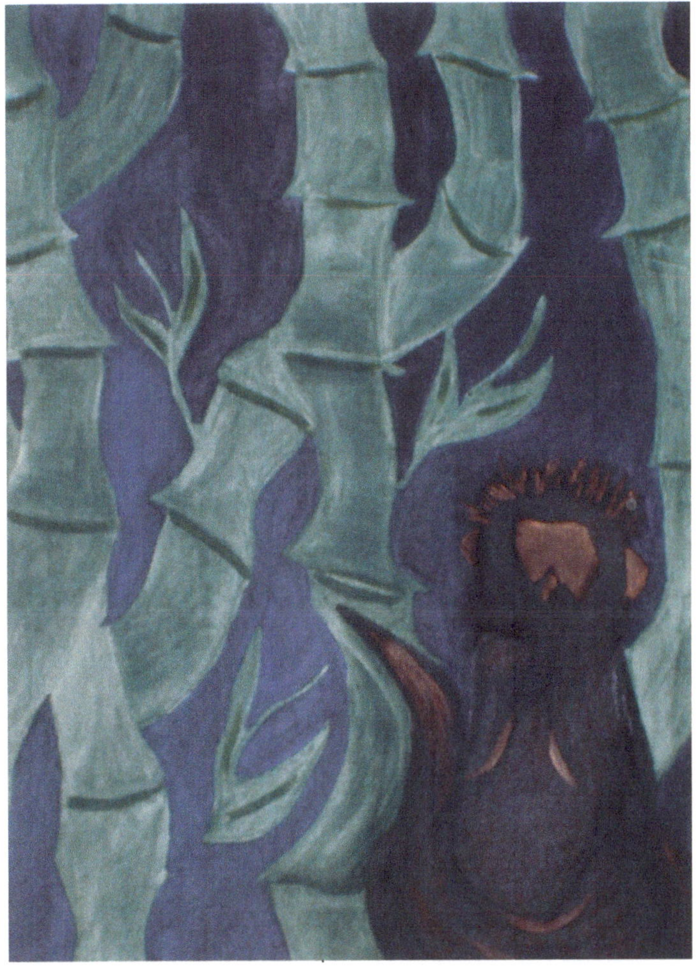

www.ingramcontent.com/pod-product-compliance
Lightning Source LLC
LaVergne TN
LVHW070506120826
845147LV00031BA/193

* 9 7 8 0 9 8 2 0 1 7 2 0 3 *